Practitioner Series

Springer
London
Berlin
Heidelberg
New York
Barcelona
Hong Kong
Milan
Paris
Santa Clara
Singapore
Tokyo

Series Editor
Russel Winder   *Kings College London, UK*

Editorial Board
Frank Bott   *UWA, Aberystwyth, UK*
Nic Holt   *ICL, Manchester, UK*
Kay Hughes   *DERA, Malvern, UK*
Elizabeth Hull   *University of Ulster, Newtownabbey (N Ireland), UK*
Richard Nance   *Virginia Tech, Blacksburg, USA*
Ray Paul   *Brunel University, Uxbridge, UK*

Other titles in this series:

The Project Management Paradigm
K. Burnett
3-540-76238-8

The Politics of Usability
L. Trenner and J. Bawa
3-540-76181-0

Electronic Commerce and Business Communications
M. Chesher and R. Kaura
3-540-19930-6

Key Java
J. Hunt and A. McManus
3-540-76259-0

Distributed Applications Engineering
I. Wijegunaratne and G. Fernandez
3-540-76210-8

Finance for IT Decision Makers
M. Blackstaff
3-540-76232-9

The Renaissance of Legacy Systems
I. Warren
1-85233-060-0

Middleware
D. Serain (Translator: I. Craig)
1-85233-011-2

Java for Practitioners
J. Hunt
1-85233-093-7

Conceptual Modeling for User Interface Development
D. Benyon, T. Green and D. Bental
1-85233-009-0

Chris Price

Computer-Based Diagnostic Systems

Springer

Chris Price
Department of Computer Science
University of Wales
Aberystwyth
SY23 3DB, UK

ISBN 3-540-76198-5 Springer-Verlag Berlin Heidelberg New York

British Library Cataloguing in Publication Data
Price, Chris
　　Computer-based diagnostic systems. - (Practitioner Series)
　　1. Expert systems (Computer science)　2. Diagnostic imaging - Data
　　processing　3. Image processing - Digital techniques
　　I. Title
　　006.3'3
　　ISBN 3540761985

Library of Congress Cataloging-in-Publication Data
Price, C. J. (Chris J.)
　　Computer-based diagnostic systems / Chris Price.
　　　　p.　　cm. -- (Practitioner series)
　　Includes bibliographical references and index.
　　ISBN 3-540-76198-5 (alk. paper)
　　1. Expert systems (Computer science)--Industrial applications.
　　I. Title. II. Series: Practitioner series (Springer-Verlag)
　　QA76.76.E95P744　1999
　　006.3'3--dc21　　　　　　　　　　　　　　　　　　　　　　　　99-36325
　　　　　　　　　　　　　　　　　　　　　　　　　　　　　　　　　　CIP

Apart from any fair dealing for the purposes of research or private study, or criticism or review, as permitted under the Copyright, Designs and Patents Act 1988, this publication may only be reproduced, stored or transmitted, in any form or by any means, with the prior permission in writing of the publishers, or in the case of reprographic reproduction in accordance with the terms of licences issued by the Copyright Licensing Agency. Enquiries concerning reproduction outside those terms should be sent to the publishers.

© Springer-Verlag London Limited 1999
Printed in Great Britain

The use of registered names, trademarks etc. in this publication does not imply, even in the absence of a specific statement, that such names are exempt from the relevant laws and regulations and therefore free for general use.

The publisher makes no representation, express or implied, with regard to the accuracy of the information contained in this book and cannot accept any legal responsibility or liability for any errors or omissions that may be made.

Typesetting: Elaine Bingham, 30 Wentworth Road, Dronfield, UK
Printed and bound at the Athenæum Press Ltd, Gateshead, Tyne and Wear, UK
34/3830-543210　Printed on acid-free paper　SPIN 10636586

Contents

Foreword	vii
Acknowledgements	ix
1. Introduction	1
1.1 Diagnostic Systems	1
1.2 Diagnosis Using Diagnostic Fault Trees	2
1.3 Building a Diagnostic System from a Diagnostic Fault Tree	4
1.4 Problems with the Diagnostic Fault Tree Approach	9
2. Disciplines for Complex Diagnostic Systems	13
2.1 Adding Structure to the Fault Tree	13
2.2 Characterizing Troubleshooting Better	18
2.3 Sources of Diagnostic Material	21
2.4 Design for Diagnosability	22
3. Tools for Complex Fault Trees	29
3.1 Graphical Fault Tree Building: A Simple Example	29
3.2 TestBench	33
3.3 GRADE™	37
3.4 Summary and Conclusions	46
4. Case-Based Diagnostic Systems	47
4.1 What Is Case-Based Reasoning?	47
4.2 CBR for Help Desk Systems	49
4.3 CBR for Complex Diagnostic Systems	54
4.4 Summary of Case-Based Reasoning	64
5. Model-Based Diagnostic Systems	65
5.1 Choosing what to Model for Model-Based Diagnosis	65
5.2 Choosing which Aspects of the Domain to Model	80
5.3 Summary and Conclusions	87
6. Applying Model-Based Diagnosis	89
6.1 RAZ'R from OCC'M	89
6.2 Automotive Diagnosis from Design Models	96
6.3 Autonomous Spacecraft Diagnosis	103

7. **Real-Time Diagnostic Systems** 109
   7.1 Characteristics of Real-Time Diagnosis 110
   7.2 Monitoring Real-Time Applications 111
   7.3 Diagnosing Real-Time Applications 115
   7.4 Commercial Real-Time Tools 118
   7.5 Tiger: Diagnosing Gas Turbines 121

Appendix 1: Full Listing of Adviser Expert System 127

Appendix 2: Details of GRAF2 Generated Programs 133
   Pascal Code Generated for Car Diagnosis Application 133
   C Code Generated for Car Diagnosis Application 136
   Execution of Text-Based Car Diagnosis Application 140
   Execution of PalmPilot-Based Car Diagnosis Application 140

Appendix 3: Further Information 143
   Chapters 1 and 2: Rule-Based Diagnostic Tools 143
   Chapter 2: Diagnosability 144
   Chapter 3: Graphically Oriented Tool Builders 144
   Chapter 4: Case-Based Reasoning Tools 145
   Chapters 5 and 6: Model-Based Reasoning Tools 146
   Chapter 7: Real-Time Diagnostic Tools 147

References 151

Index 155

Foreword

The world is full of faults. Some products develop faults as they are used, some products have faults from the moment of manufacture. Some faults lead to the unusability of a product, some faults can be ignored. There are even some products that have faults that are never actually discovered because they are never exposed by use.

Even though we live in what many have called the "Disposable Society", there are many products for which, when a fault is discovered, we want there to be a mechanism of repair so that we can continue to use the product. In all such cases, we need to be able to detect and understand the fault (or faults) if we are to remove it (or them). Consider, for example washing machines, cars, aeroplanes, computers, software. These products are too costly to be "disposable". When something goes wrong, we expect to be able to diagnose the fault and repair it.

Detection of a *potential* fault in a product is (usually) easy: use of the product has led to an unexpected behaviour by the product. A person's immediate reaction in such a situation is often that there is a fault in the product. Usually the fault is actually with the operator – the person failed to understand the operation of the product in the way the manufacturer intended. Of course, many would argue that this is actually an indirect fault of the product (or at least its documentation) since it allowed the user to build an incorrect understanding of the product. Whether the fault is user error or an actual fault in the product, the situation needs to be understood by the user so that the appropriate action can be taken.

End users need some sort of support tool to help them understand the situation and decide whether the fault is caused by their own improper use of the product or whether there is a need to employ a trained technician. Moreover, products are becoming increasingly complex so even the trained technicians, who are usually good at diagnosis and repair, can benefit from decision support tools other than their own memory and training.

Until recently, most diagnostic systems have been document-based. Most people have experience of the diagnostic tables that car manufacturers and computer manufacturers put into the documentation for their products. However, as computer systems become increasingly used and increasingly mobile, the opportunities for using computer-based systems for diagnosis increase. More usually this implies use by the trained technician but can also be for initial user diagnosis. These tools invariably use knowledge-based system technology (rule-based, case-based and model-based reasoning) and, increasingly, hypertext document technology for their implementation.

So far, we have assumed that it is human constructed products that are in need of diagnostic support tools. There are other areas in which faults and diagnosis are important: medicine, for example. However, as is pointed out very early on in this book, there is a very significant difference between medical diagnosis and the diagnosis of faults in products. In medicine, intervention techniques are almost a last resort for diagnosis. As Price points out "you cannot replace parts of a human to test hypotheses about what is faulty". Conversely, for diagnosis of products, intervention (usually the replacement of parts) is an integral part of the diagnostic approach. In effect, diagnosis and repair are more integrally linked when dealing with constructed products.

Thus, the techniques and decision-making processes employed when using intervention as a diagnostic strategy are very different compared to those used otherwise, such as in medicine. This book concentrates on intervention enabled techniques. It covers the major algorithms and implementation techniques. The book does not cover the user interface issues, this would be a separate book in its own right, it stays very much with the core diagnostic system itself. Likewise there is no coverage of call centre issues since this is not a book on the sociological – HCI – management aspects of diagnostic systems.

This is very much a book for the developer or potential developer of diagnostic systems for constructed artefacts. It presents an overview of the technology including the major products available. The important approaches are covered with practical, realistic examples and guidelines for the systems developer. This is a book for the working practitioner. Of course it could, quite reasonably, see use as a "set text" for a final year option in a university degree programme but this was not the main target audience in its construction. If you are, or will be, developing diagnostic systems, or perhaps you are just interested in how such systems are developed in practice, then this book is for you.

Russel Winder

Acknowledgements

This book could not have been written without the input of many people experienced in diagnosis and in building diagnostic systems. Where this book contains useful material, it is based on their experience; where it is wrong, it is because I have learned their lessons imperfectly.

Those who have helped me to understand the diagnostic process, especially:

- Ossie Hornsby of ICI Billingham, for showing me how complex modern processing plants could be, and how necessary good alarm reporting systems are.
- Mike Bell, Stefek Zaba and Jon Young, for working with me to build the SAGE expert system shell.
- Jim Rice, now at Stanford University, for giving me my first exposure to automated diagnosis when we both worked at SPL International and he was building diagnostic systems for Kodak.
- Paddy, shift supervisor at the Reprocessing Plant in Sellafield, for patiently explaining the complexity of many diagnostic decisions and the necessity for correctness in difficult situations.
- Johan de Kleer and Brian Williams for writing model-based diagnosis papers that inspired me and many others to try building model-based diagnostic systems.
- All the partners on the Vehicle Model Based Diagnosis project for making diagnosis interesting for me again, after several years working on design analysis instead.

Those who have supported the writing of this book:

- John Hunt deserves a special mention: this book came out of some seminars that we gave at the British Computer Society Expert Systems conferences. If he hadn't been too busy writing Java books, it would have been a joint authored book.
- Peter Struss and Oskar Dressler of OCC'M, for providing information on the RAZ'R system and the ABS application.
- Rob Milne of Intelligent Applications for providing Tiger material.
- Roy Bonney and Adrian Dore of GenRad for providing a demonstration copy of GRADE and for answering my questions.

- Rob Wylie of National Research Council of Canada for providing information on the Air Canada application.
- Mark Lee of UW Aberystwyth, amid much encouragement over the years, for reading several drafts of the book.
- George Coghill and Richard Shipman of UW Aberystwyth, and Andrew Parr of Co-Steel, for reading and commenting on the final draft.
- Tom Bartlett, while an MSc student at Aberystwyth, for adding Palm-Pilot code to my GRAF2 program.

Those who have supported me during the gestation of this book:

- Ann, Bethan and John, for allowing me to disappear to the computer instead of being a family member occasionally.
- My parents and wider family, for their love and support throughout my life.
- All the members of the Department of Computer Science at UW Aberystwyth, for making it a great place to work.
- The Creator and Sustainer of us all, in whose image we all create. Like Him, when we see faults in our creation, we perform diagnosis and take action.

1. Introduction

1.1 Diagnostic Systems

Diagnostic systems are among the most successful applications of knowledge-based systems (KBS) technology. This is true both in terms of the number of applications built, and in terms of the benefits that such systems bring.

This book addresses the issue of the best way to build effective diagnostic systems for different types of diagnostic problem. Ten years ago, this would not have been much of an issue – there was really only one solution for building diagnostic systems: such systems were built using an expert system shell or a programming language. However, there are now several good ways of building diagnostic systems and the appropriate solution will depend on the characteristics of the specific diagnostic problem.

The book is limited to the issue of building diagnostic systems for devices designed by humans. Medical diagnosis is an important area, but has some significant differences from diagnosis of devices designed by humans: for example, in medical diagnosis, part replacement to prove malfunction is not often an appropriate diagnostic test, whereas it is a standard strategy in many areas of device diagnosis. Because of this, fuzzy reasoning has a much higher profile in medical diagnosis, whereas device diagnosis is more likely to use tests to provide exact answers.

Given that the book shows how to build *effective* diagnostic systems, then it is appropriate to consider what the measure of an effective diagnostic system is. There are a number of important factors to consider.

- *Efficient construction.* Is the diagnostic system being implemented in the most efficient way, at the lowest cost, in the minimum time necessary?

- *Reasonable maintainability.* Can the diagnostic system be maintained at the lowest cost, given that the device being diagnosed is likely to change over time, and new diagnostic problems will be discovered as the device is used?

- *Adequate coverage.* Does the diagnostic system provide diagnoses for a reasonable percentage of the faults that occur? Ideally, the requirement would be for 100 per cent coverage, but in practice, coverage is traded against system construction cost.

- *Correct answers.* For what proportion of faults that it covers does the system give the correct answer? Again, the ideal requirement is 100 per cent of answers correct.
- *Minimum effort from the user.* Users do not appreciate performing unnecessary tests or providing irrelevant information. Diagnostic systems should aim to demand the least information necessary from the user.
- *Appropriate response time.* The acid test here is: does the diagnostic system provide an answer when it is needed? For some particularly demanding applications, that might be within milliseconds, but for many applications, it is of the order of a small number of seconds.
- *Good cost/benefit ratio for diagnosis.* How this is calculated is an issue for the company evaluating whether to build a particular diagnostic application, but the main costs are likely to be implementation, maintenance and distribution of the diagnostic system. The main benefits tend to be in terms of savings in engineer time (fewer hours per correct diagnosis made) and in improved device availability or reduced downtime.

Diagnostic problems vary widely, and the differences between problems will affect the balance between the criteria discussed above. For example, in a safety critical process control application, say a chemical processing plant, the cost/benefit ratio might be irrelevant compared with the need to provide correct answers within a tight timeframe.

This book gives examples of different solutions to the problem of building effective diagnostic systems, and shows the types of diagnostic problems for which each solution is appropriate. Presented with a new diagnostic problem, the book should enable the reader to decide on an appropriate strategy for building a diagnostic system to aid troubleshooting of that diagnostic problem.

There are a number of simple tools and demonstration systems referred to in the rest of the book. The material can be obtained via the World Wide Web and run on the reader's own machine. In a few cases, the material merely provides links to commercial demonstrations. The intention of all the material is that it should make the book easier to understand where the reader does not have access to the commercial tools, or for teaching the material to an undergraduate class. The Web address for obtaining software and other material linked to the book is "http:/www.aber.ac.uk/~cjp/diagnosticbook/". Appendix 3 provides details of the Web site and of companies active in diagnostic systems technology.

1.2 Diagnosis Using Diagnostic Fault Trees

One of the main ways in which engineers have represented a diagnostic strategy is by using diagnostic fault trees. Diagnostic fault trees are also a convenient way of thinking about building diagnostic systems.

Introduction   3

- *They can be easily understood.* How to interpret a diagnostic tree can easily be explained to anyone who has not seen one before.

- *They are used by engineers to describe troubleshooting procedures.* They are in a format that will already be understandable to engineers who spend their days performing diagnostic tests. Where the diagnostic system is being built by someone other than an expert diagnostician, the diagnostic fault trees will be a good way of sharing knowledge between the constructor of the diagnostic system and the diagnosticians.

- *They can represent a wide range of diagnostic problems.* Even where there is some reason for not representing a diagnostic problem as a diagnostic fault tree (for example, because the tree is too large to represent or because the tree will change depending on answers to previous questions), it can still be helpful to think of the problem in terms of diagnostic fault trees.

The rest of this book uses diagnostic fault trees as a common representation for discussing different ways of approaching diagnosis, and shows how the qualities of the diagnostic tree affect the choice of technology for building the diagnostic system effectively. Some of the approaches are closer to diagnostic fault trees than others, but it is hoped that in all cases the comparison with diagnostic fault trees will shed light on the characteristics of the diagnostic system being built.

This chapter starts the process by illustrating the simplest solution: direct implementation of the diagnostic tree in a programming language or an expert system shell. This is followed by a discussion of the benefits and shortcomings of this approach for particular types of trees, and an outline of the types of diagnostic system addressed in the rest of the book, each of which addresses one or more of these shortcomings.

Performing diagnosis with a diagnostic fault tree such as the one shown in Figure 1.1 is done in the following way:

>The user starts at the top of the tree.
>When the user is at a diamond shaped node, the test should be applied.
>>If the answer to the test is "Yes",
>>>then the user follows the left path to the next node.
>>If the answer to the test is "No",
>>>then the user follows the right path to the next node.
>When the user reaches a rectangular node, this is a leaf node, and contains the diagnosis.

The diagnostic fault tree in Figure 1.1 is a very simple example for illustration purposes, and has been chosen because it is likely to be familiar to most readers. A realistic system for diagnosing problems in starting a car would need to consider many more possible faults, and would need to provide much more detail about how to perform tests and how to carry out repairs.

If the diagnostic fault tree traversal algorithm just stated is applied to the diagnostic fault tree in Figure 1.1, then it might result in a tree traversal as follows:

Test to see whether the car starts (turn the ignition):
   Answer is "no" – follow the right hand branch

Test whether the starter motor turns (turn ignition and listen):
   Answer is "no" – follow the right hand branch

Test whether headlights are working OK (turn headlights on and observe):
   Answer is "no" – follow the right hand branch

Algorithm has reached a leaf node:
   Problem is flat battery. Take appropriate repair action.

In order to draw a diagnostic fault tree such as that in Figure 1.1, you must decide what is the first diagnostic test to be done, and draw it at the top of the tree. The possible next actions or questions are drawn beneath it, linked by the answers that lead to those actions or questions. In the example shown, only yes/no questions are used, but the same technique can be used for more complex sets of answers.

This section has shown how a user might build and use a graphical diagnostic fault tree by hand. The next section will discuss automation of the process of traversing the diagnostic fault tree. This is done by building a diagnostic system that represents and traverses the tree.

1.3 Building a Diagnostic System from a Diagnostic Fault Tree

A diagnostic fault tree of the kind illustrated in Figure 1.1 can be easily encoded using an expert systems shell. It could also be implemented in a conventional programming language such as Pascal or C (as will be shown in Chapter 3, where a graphical diagnostic fault tree builder is used to generate Pascal code for the same simple example).

An expert system shell has some advantages over a conventional programming language when hand-crafting a diagnostic system:

- *Extra features.* The shell used in the example provides features other than just asking questions: it allows the user to retract answers; to enquire why a question is being asked; and to ask for further clarification of the meaning of questions.

- *Avoidance of unnecessary questions.* Shells usually do not ask for information that has already been given. This can avoid asking for repetition of a test that has already been carried out.

- *Better quality of interface.* The example shown is of the simplest version of the shell's interface. It also has an optional Windows interface, bringing up questions in separate dialog boxes allowing answers via mouse clicks. The code in Appendix 1 can produce a Windows-friendly interface automatically without the need to write lots of graphical user interface code.

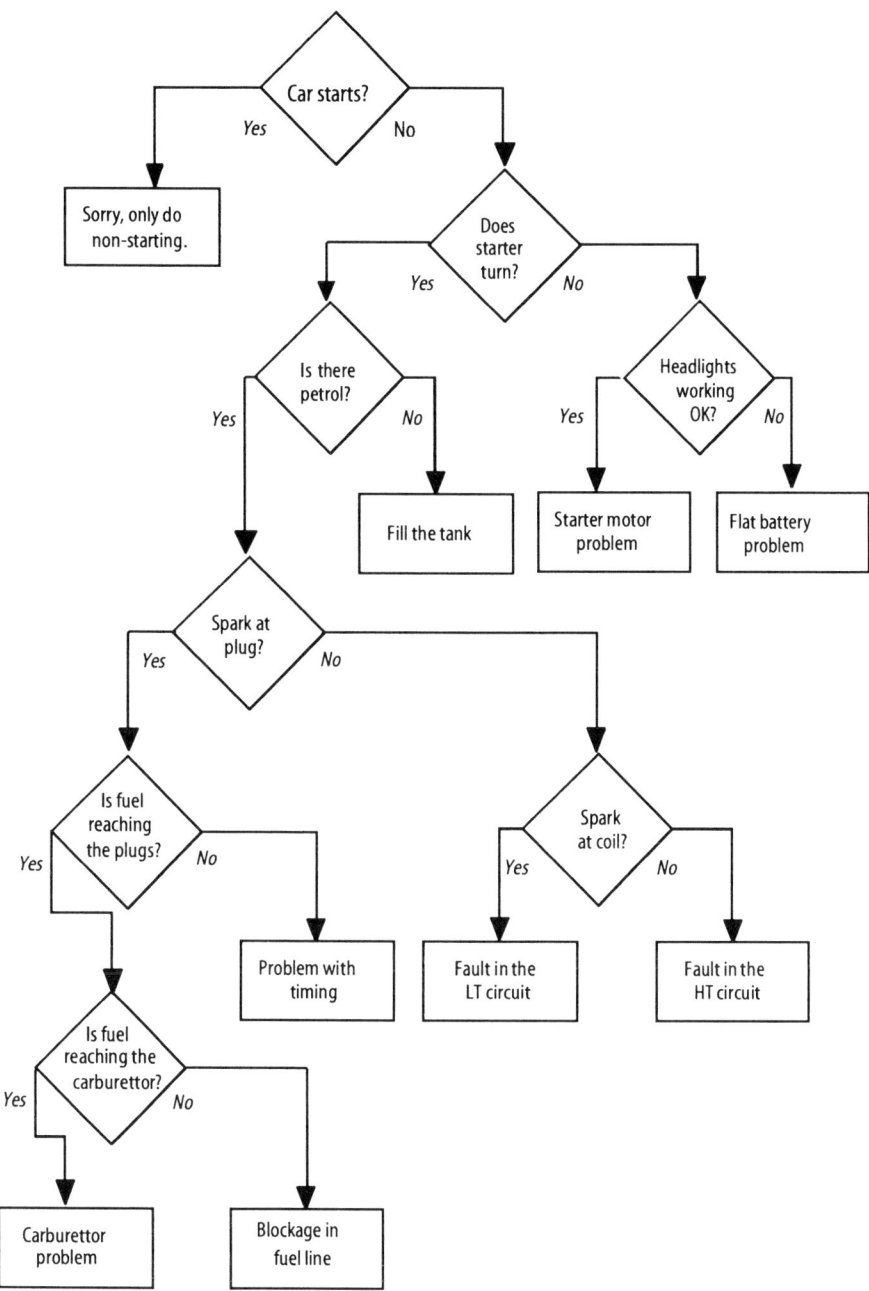

Fig. 1.1 A simple diagnostic fault tree.

The advantages of using a shell over a conventional programming language are much reduced when using a graphical diagnostic system builder to generate the diagnostic system in the conventional language, as shown in Chapter 3. This is because the repetitive coding to enable extra user interface features and to exclude unnecessary tests can be automatically generated by the graphical diagnostic system builder.

The example expert system code shown is implemented in the expert system shell, Adviser, and a full listing and example runs of the system are given in Appendix 1. In order to illustrate how the system is implemented, short extracts from the code and a short example of running the system will be given here.

Adviser is a backward-chaining expert system shell: given a goal to evaluate, it will attempt to execute rules or ask questions to obtain that goal. Its top level of control is imperative; it has a list of actions to execute, and it will first evaluate their precondition if any, and if the precondition is true, then it will carry out the action.

The example diagnostic system has only two possible actions. If the car will not start (discerned by asking the user), then the diagnostic system finds a value for the string "answer" and prints a piece of advice. If the car will start, then the diagnostic system refuses to help.

```
ACTION main_advice : "This action gives the diagnostic advice."
   PROVIDED NOT(car_starts)
   ADVISE "!2NThe problem seems to be ", answer, "!3N"

ACTION preliminary_reject: "Reject at preliminary conditions."
   PROVIDED car_starts
   ADVISE "!5N This system is only designed for",
      "!N finding faults in cars that won't start."

ASSERTION car_starts : "User does not have a suitable problem"
   DEFAULT FALSE
QUESTION ask_if_car_starts: ""
   OBTAIN car_starts YESNO
   WITH "Try to start your car: did it start?"
   WHY "The system is only designed for no start problems."
```

This top node of the diagnostic fault tree is dealt with specially, but the rest of the tree is all dealt with by returning a string containing a description of the problem and what to do about it. These literal strings are the leaf nodes of the tree, and look like the following example.

```
CONSTANT STRING battery_fault = "a flat battery".
   + "!2N Recharge the battery and figure out"
   + "why it was flat (lights on, old battery etc)."
```

The branching body of the tree is dealt with by representing each question node as a string variable that will get its value from one of two other strings depending on the answer to a question. For example, the node just below the top of the car diagnostic fault tree in Figure 1.1 is dealt with in the following way:

Introduction

```
STRING answer : "Does the starter turn"
RULE a_answer : ""
   answer IS fuel_or_ign_fault
   PROVIDED q_engine_turns
      ALSO answer IS st_motor_or_battery_fault
   PROVIDED NOT(q_engine_turns)
```

The assertion q_engine_turns is given a value by asking the user whether the engine turns, as follows. If the engine turns slowly, it is taken as a "No" answer.

```
ASSERTION q_engine_turns: ""
QUESTION ask_if_engine_turns: ""
   ANSWERS q_engine_turns
      CHOICE "No"              : FALSE
      CHOICE "Yes, but slowly": FALSE
      CHOICE "Yes, normally"   : TRUE
   WITH "Does the engine turn over?"
```

Each branching point in the tree is implemented in the same way as above. For example, the branch below to the right of the one given above is implemented as follows:

```
STRING st_motor_or_battery_fault: ""
RULE a_st_motor_or_battery_fault: ""
   st_motor_or_battery_fault IS st_motor_fault
   PROVIDED NOT(q_battery_flat)
      ALSO st_motor_or_battery_fault IS battery_fault
   PROVIDED (q_battery_flat)
```

When this code is executed in Adviser, then a dialogue of the following type occurs. Bold type is used to indicate the answers typed by the user.

This expert system diagnoses car problems,

Try to start your car: did it start?
(You may answer Yes or No): **n**

Does the engine turn over?
1. No
2. Yes, but slowly
3. Yes, normally
(Please make your choice): **1**

How bright are the headlamps?
1. No light
2. Dim
3. Normal brightness
(Please make your choice): **1**

The problem seems to be a flat battery.

Recharge the battery and figure out why it was flat (lights on, old battery etc).

It is evident that the run of the Adviser expert system shown is equivalent to the algorithm given for following the paper-based diagnostic fault tree. The advantages for the user over using a diagnostic fault tree pictured on a piece of paper are:

- the diagnostic system keeps track of how far the traversal of the tree has progressed;
- for a tree that is too large to fit on one piece of paper (most realistic trees are larger than that), the diagnostic system handles the complexity of moving between sheets of paper;
- much more test information can be included in the expert system than can be done on a piece of paper;
- much more repair information can be included in the expert system than can be done on a piece of paper;
- more complex nodes can be included in the expert system. This has not been done in the above example, but it is possible to branch more than two ways. For example, you could ask the user for a numeric value and branch three or four ways depending on the result of the test. Such branches can be very complex to draw on paper.

This approach also has several advantages as a way of building diagnostic systems:

- *Easy implementation.* It provides a clear strategy for implementing a diagnostic system like the one illustrated in Adviser, and so a diagnostic fault tree can be encoded in a straightforward manner. Without such a strategy, building rules can be difficult and counter-intuitive.
- *Reasonable maintainability.* Inserting extra nodes into the diagnostic fault tree is fairly easy to do. In the case of the Adviser expert system shown, it would mean editing one rule and adding a new rule (to insert the new branch), and adding a new assertion and question (to add the new node).
- *Extendibility.* The representation used here can be extended. As well as having more complex branches in the tree, it is possible to have more complex types of advice. Where repair is complicated to carry out, further expert system code can be written which asks questions and takes the user through a complex repair procedure.
- *Clear order for asking questions.* A major advantage of implementing an expert system in this manner using a backward chaining expert system shell is that the tree gives you an explicit order of investigation for faults, just as the original diagnostic fault tree on paper did. This order is decided by the person building the system, and can be based on a number of different factors, for example:
    - cost of performing tests
    - likelihood of the fault occurring
    - repercussions of the fault occurring

The explicit ordering of investigation means that the diagnostic system can be constructed so that the human diagnosticians using the system make the best use of their time. This advantage can be quite hard to reproduce in some other kinds of diagnostic systems. It is also important for effective maintenance of the diagnostic system, as it makes it easy to understand and control what the system does.

This simple expert system diagnostic fault tree approach has been in use for more than ten years. The approach has been applied to many diagnostic problems and works well, although the task of generating the expert system code for a large diagnostic system can involve a lot of work. However the approach has its problems for many diagnostic applications, and the next section explores the kinds of problems that can occur.

1.4 Problems with the Diagnostic Fault Tree Approach

It has been suggested in this chapter that a good approach to building a diagnostic system is to think of the diagnostic process as a diagnostic fault tree, perhaps actually draw the tree on a piece of paper, and then encode the diagnostic fault tree in an expert system shell.

There are many diagnostic problems for which this approach is inadequate. In many cases, the difficulties with using the diagnostic fault tree approach can be identified by thinking about what the diagnostic fault tree for a system would look like. This section will discuss the different types of difficulties that can occur, and outline the solutions to these difficulties that are discussed in the rest of the book.

1.4.1 The Diagnostic Fault Tree Can Get Very Large

It is difficult to visualize a very large diagnostic fault tree. When a tree can be depicted on a single sheet of paper (or on several sheets stuck together), then it is easy to understand what is happening.

As the tree becomes larger, it gets difficult to maintain the drawing of the diagnostic fault tree, let alone any expert system code implemented from it, and the size of the problem can make the developers lose control of the diagnostic system.

Another challenge with large diagnostic fault trees is keeping track of all the leaves and branches in the tree. It becomes difficult to tell whether all of the diagnostic tree has been drawn (whether all possible problems have been dealt with), or whether a few branches have been lost.

Because the tree is so big, it is very difficult to decide where a particular test or set of tests should be placed in the tree. This problem is even worse where some portions of the tree are very repetitive. For example, in a diagnostic system for the door-locking system of a car, it would be a great waste of effort to implement part of the diagnostic fault tree four or five times (once for each door-locking mechanism).

There are several possible solutions to the difficulties caused by complexity of the diagnostic fault tree. The main solutions are described in Chapters 2 and 3. It is possible to impose a higher level control structure on the diagnostic fault tree to help deal with the complexity, or to use graphical tools to describe the diagnostic fault tree. Such tools generate the diagnostic system code from pictures, and so enable the user to edit graphical diagnostic fault trees rather than editing code directly. If the complex diagnostic fault tree consists of many diagnoses that do not change radically over time then either of these strategies will work reasonably well.

1.4.2 The Diagnostic Fault Tree is New (and Empty)

This is a common problem when a new device is being built for the first time. For example, when a computer manufacturer is about to produce a brand new machine, they will want a diagnostic system available for their engineers as soon as the first machine is delivered to a customer. How can a diagnostic fault tree be drawn when there is no previous experience of diagnosing the device?

A partial solution is presented in Chapter 2, where other sources for diagnostic material are identified. Although there might be no experience of diagnosing this device, there is a wealth of more general experience that can be employed in order to build the diagnostic system.

A second possibility is the use of case-based reasoning, If there is a record of diagnostic problems and fixes for previous similar devices, then perhaps that information can be used for diagnosing the new device. Chapter 4 will describe the diagnostic case-based reasoning systems.

A third possibility is the use of model-based reasoning. Design information can be used to automate the construction of the diagnostic fault tree. Chapters 5 and 6 will describe different uses of models for the construction of diagnostic systems.

1.4.3 The Diagnostic Fault Tree Changes Frequently

A common problem is where many different variants on a device are being made to meet the demands of different customers. Each variant of the device might need a slightly different version of the diagnostic system. This might be because the devices are expensive (such as chemical plants), and each one is customized to the user. It might be because the devices have different markets (such as cars, where different countries have different legal requirements). How can you build each of those variant systems as efficiently as possible?

At one level, the disciplines discussed in Chapter 2 can help. Partitioning the diagnostic fault tree can make it easier to fit together the right set of partitions for a particular variant of a device. A better solution is the automated use of design information in model-based diagnosis: given the design for this particular variant, the correct diagnostic fault tree can be automatically generated. It is for this type of diagnostic problem that model-based diagnosis has the greatest promise.

1.4.4 The Diagnostic Fault Tree is Really a Small Forest of Different Species of Tree

The classic example of this is the computer help desk situation. Computer users have many different types of problem, and the problems are often not really related to each other. The users can have problems with:

- *software* – not knowing what commands to give, running the wrong version, running it on the wrong computer, not having the right files, not having the right permissions;
- *different pieces of local hardware* – broken computers, unplugged keyboards, disconnected monitors;
- *network* – local computer not connected, hub down, repeater broken, remote file store unavailable, printer software malfunctioning, printer unavailable.

Each of these problem areas can be considered as separate trees. In fact, the area of "software problems" might need breaking down into more than one tree. Some of the software problems are caused by software malfunctioning, and others are problems caused by the user's ignorance. One of the main diagnostic challenges for a computer help desk is to distinguish between those two possibilities.

However, the different problem areas are all interlinked at the symptom level. For example, if the user is having a problem printing a file, the cause of the problem could be in any of the areas mentioned above. How do you find the right tree? Usually, the user's description of the problem will guide diagnosis towards one area rather than another, and questions can be used to focus the diagnosis further. Case-based reasoning provides a good way of collecting diverse diagnostic information into a more coherent system.

1.4.5 Continuous Diagnosis is Needed

The diagnostic fault tree approach is suited to single-shot diagnosis: a device has broken and it needs to be fixed. A set of tests can be carried out in sequence, where the results of tests can be seen immediately, and it is clear when the device has been repaired.

There is another type of diagnostic system for which the diagnostic fault tree approach is not so appropriate. Continuous monitoring and diagnostic systems that need to take appropriate action when something goes wrong are really rather different from the kinds of tree that we have been talking about, and need to be dealt with differently.

For the most part, this book will be dealing with "single-shot" diagnostic systems, as many applications can be dealt with in that way, but Chapter 7 will address the construction of continuous real-time diagnostic systems.

2. Disciplines for Complex Diagnostic Systems

It was observed in Chapter 1 that the implementation and maintenance of a diagnostic fault tree becomes more difficult as the size of the tree increases. This chapter considers how imposing a higher level structure on the diagnostic fault tree can compensate for the effect of complexity. It provides guidance for selecting such a higher level structure, based on the different tasks that make up troubleshooting.

Section 2.1 shows how an expert system can be partitioned in order to make it easier to understand and maintain. Section 2.2 considers the wider issues raised by the examples in Section 2.1. It provides a characterization of the range of tasks needed to perform diagnosis. Understanding the different tasks involved in diagnosis will be useful whatever type of technology is being used to build a diagnostic system. When a diagnostic system is being constructed, the builders should make sure that they use whatever information is available. Section 2.3 discusses the different sources of information and experience for building diagnostic systems.

Section 2.4 considers a complementary approach, designing a product from the outset to make diagnosis as effective as possible. Diagnostic systems are often built after a device has been designed and manufactured. More effective diagnostic systems can often be constructed if diagnostic issues are considered when the device is being designed. This section of the chapter deals with the issues of designing systems so that they can be easily diagnosed.

2.1 Adding Structure to the Fault Tree

There is a problem with extending the kind of expert system shown in Chapter 1 for the simple car diagnosis. Even at that size, it can be difficult to follow the code representing the logic of the tree. When a fault tree gets large, it can be developed more efficiently if it is arranged into sensible pieces that are fairly separate from each other. The main criterion for breaking up the tree into subtrees should be that each subtree is coherent: it maps onto problems with some particular area of the device, or onto problems of a particular kind.

This strategy works quite well where there is not too much of an overlap between the different parts of the tree. Essentially this strategy involves building many simpler diagnostic systems instead of one big complex one. The method of carrying out this strategy is to identify significant tests that split the tree into coherent parts, and treat each part as a separate tree. This strategy is illustrated in Figure 2.1, where there might be many small fault trees at the bottom of the picture, and control is passed to one of them depending on which of the possible distinguishing symptoms are observed.

The use of structure to control the complexity of the diagnostic system is best illustrated by giving some examples of how it might be done for specific problems.

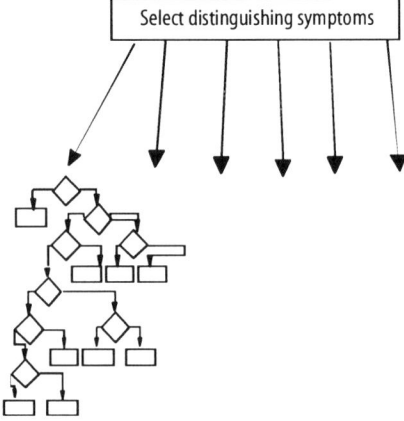

Fig. 2.1 Arrangement of diagnostic system into small fault trees.

2.1.1 Adding Structure, Example 1: Car Diagnosis Revisited

For the car example shown in Chapter 1, the fault tree that was shown would not be a complete diagnostic system. It is more like a high level set of tests used to identify the problem in more detail. For example, having identified that the problem is in the low-tension circuit rather than the high-tension circuit or the battery, it would be necessary to carry out some more specific tests to identify the problem component. The more specific tests concerned with the low-tension circuit could be arranged into a sensible lower-level fault tree.

2.1.2 Adding Structure, Example 2: Metal Insertion Machine

This is an example of a practical diagnostic system in use in industry where the fault tree would be unmanageable if it was built as a single tree. The purpose of the diagnostic system is to solve problems on electro-mechanical machines used to insert metal terminals and screws into a plastic block, making an electrical connector block. The final component produced is pictured in Figure 2.2.

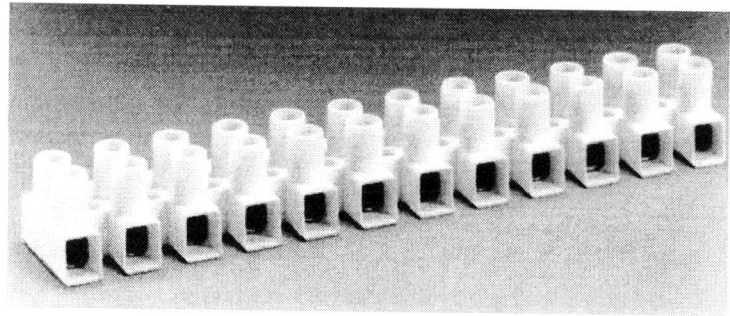

Fig. 2.2 Electrical connector block assembled by insertion machine.

This process can go wrong in many different ways. The overall system contains several hundred possible problems, on two different types of machine (one type of machine, the Blosch, uses pneumatics to move parts and so has a completely different set of reasons why problems can occur than the other, the Sortimat, which is purely electromechanical).

The diagnostic system applies the approach pictured in Figure 2.1, asking two questions at the start in order to use high-level information to focus on one of 17 subsystems, each containing a small fault subtree of perhaps 10 or 20 possible problems. This is achieved by the following top-level imperative code, written in Adviser again:

```
// The following action asks a big menu question and branches to an
// area whose name is made up of the problem type plus machine type
// For example: Inverted_insert_area_blosch

ACTION More_specific_investigation: "Start the right sub-area"
   COMMAND "CONSIDER " + main_problem + "_area_" + Machine_type
```

This action causes the system to ask two questions to obtain values for the strings "main_problem" and "machine_type". Once this has been done, the system will execute a command of the format "CONSIDER <main_problem>_area_<machine_type>". For example, in the first run of the system listed below, the system executes "CONSIDER insert_failure_area_sortimat". This area is an encapsulated part of the diagnostic system that just looks at problems to do with insertion failures on Sortimat machines. Within each area, the code looks very similar in style to that shown for the car diagnosis example in Chapter 1.

The first question lists the main symptoms that can occur. They are ordered so that the more important symptoms are listed first, so that the user will choose the more significant symptoms where more than one symptom is present.

```
STRING Main_problem: "First find out the type of fault seen"
QUESTION Main_question: "Identify general problem area"
            ANSWERS                           Main_Problem
   CHOICE "Machine stops running or fails to start"   : "Bust"
   CHOICE "Failure to pick up or to feed part"        : "Feed_failure"
   CHOICE "Fails to put insert into component"       : "Insert_failure"
```

```
        CHOICE "Insert put in upside down"              : "Inverted_insert"
        CHOICE "Insert missing"                         : "Missing_insert"
        CHOICE "Screws missing"                         : "Missing_screw"
        CHOICE "Problems with placing screws in insert" : "Screw_problem"
        CHOICE "Screws wrong height"                    : "Screw_height"
        CHOICE "Damaged assemblies on Blosch"           : "Blosch_damage"
    WITH "Which sort of problem is there with the machine? "
    MORE "!N First find out the type of fault on the machine. ",
         "!N Make sure that you check the fault for yourself, ",
         "!N rather than just relying on what the operator tells you"
```

The second question asks which kind of machine has the problem. This is necessary because only some of the problem types are shared between the two types of machines.

```
    STRING Machine_type: "Is it a Blosch or a Sortimat problem"
    DEFAULT "Sortimat"
    QUESTION Machine_type_question: ""
        ANSWERS             Machine_type
        CHOICE "Sortimat"   : "Sortimat"
        CHOICE "Blosch"     : "Blosch"
    WITH "Which kind of insert machine are you trying to diagnose? "
```

Once the first two questions have been asked, the diagnostic system invokes a diagnostic fault tree similar to the one shown in Chapter 1, but only for the small set of possibilities that match the symptoms.

The following listing shows two example runs of the insertion machine diagnostic system.

```
    Mechanical insert machine diagnosis assistant. This system guides the
    diagnosis of problems on the company's six mechanical insert machines.

    For faults where the machine is still running, it is a good idea to
    watch it working for a few minutes to get a clear picture of what is
    happening, rather than relying on someone else's report of what is
    happening.

    Which sort of problem is there with the machine?
    1. Machine stops running or fails to start
    2. Failure to pick up or to feed part
    3. Fails to put insert into component
    4. Insert put in upside down
    5. Insert missing
    6. Screws missing
    7. Problems with placing screws in insert
    8. Screws wrong height
    9. Damaged assemblies on Blosch
    (Please make your choice): 3

    Which kind of insert machine are you trying to diagnose?
    1. Sortimat
    2. Blosch
    (Please make your choice): 1
```

Try increasing the insert bowl feed rate.
Did that help? **n**

Is the insert bowl tooling damaged or worn? **n**

Is the insert track out of alignment? **n**

Is the insert track feed rate wrong? **n**

Is the insert head out of position? **n**

Is the insert head spring tension wrong? **n**

Is the insert head front plate either too tight or too loose? **n**

Is the top cover pulling or pushing the housings as it positions them? **y**

Slacken the cap heads, and cycle through for two housings
to make sure OK, and then tighten.

Would you like to try out another problem?
(You may answer Yes or No): **y**

Which sort of problem is there with the machine?
1. Machine stops running or fails to start
2. Failure to pick up or to feed part
3. Fails to put insert into component
4. Insert put in upside down
5. Insert missing
6. Screws missing
7. Problems with placing screws in insert
8. Screws wrong height
9. Damaged assemblies on Blosch
(Please make your choice): **3**

Which kind of insert machine are you trying to diagnose?
1. Sortimat
2. Blosch
(Please make your choice): **2**

Do the housings being fed in have flash or missing chimneys? **n**

Does the magazine contain the wrong housings (some types of housing
are similar in appearance)? **n**

Turn machine off.

Check insert machine / track alignment and push inserts
Is there any resistance? **y**

The insert head is out of adjustment.
Adjust it until the inserts move freely.

Would you like to try out another problem?
(You may answer Yes or No): **n**

In some diagnostic systems, the criteria for splitting the tree can be more complex than the couple of questions needed in the insertion machine example, but the principle is good for more complex systems: divide and conquer the large problem by breaking it into coherent pieces of a manageable size.

This kind of strategy for building large diagnostic systems works for almost any large device, for example cars, elevators or coal-cutting machines.

It is less successful for rapidly changing fault trees. Power networks or telecommunications networks, for example, do not fit this strategy very well, because the diagnostic strategy will change as the topology of the network changes.

The next section considers the different subtasks that are involved in diagnosis, as they provide a sensible way of breaking down the diagnostic task into more manageable chunks.

2.2 Characterizing Troubleshooting Better

An understanding of the different tasks being carried out in troubleshooting is useful in order to understand better how to decompose fault trees efficiently. The whole of the troubleshooting task can be described as being made up of five subtasks:

- problem identification;
- fault localization;
- fault identification;
- fault diagnosis;
- repair.

These subtasks are best illustrated by considering examples of what they involve in particular troubleshooting tasks.

2.2.1 Diagnostic Subtasks, Example 1: Fertilizer Manufacturing Plant

Consider a fertilizer manufacturing chemical plant with a problem that flow through a set of pipes does not result in an expected increase in volume in an adjacent tank. The five subtasks of troubleshooting might be carried out as follows:

- *Problem identification.* The fertilizer manufacturing plant will have many sensors monitoring pressures, temperatures, volume and flow of liquid in the plant. A problem would be identified by one of the readings going outside a permitted range, or by a relationship between readings being violated, such as the level in one tank decreasing without the level in a connected tank increasing as expected (perhaps due to a leak).

- *Fault localization.* Having identified that there is a problem, it is possible to restrict the possible causes for the problem. Where liquid flow through a set of pipes does not result in an expected increase in volume in a tank, then the problem can probably only be caused by:
  - a faulty flow sensor or volume sensor;
  - leakage in the set of pipes;
  - leakage in/unexpected flow from the vessel.

  For the fertilizer manufacturing plant, some preliminary actions might be taken at this point in some cases, if there is a strong likelihood of a liquid leak. For example, a plant shutdown might be initiated as a precautionary measure.

- *Fault identification.* Once the fault has been localized, the next step is to try to identify the type of fault that exists. The two types mentioned are leakages and faulty sensor readings. This might be done by using further sensor readings if they are available. For example, information about liquid flow into the region of plant where the previous flow reading was taken might indicate whether the flow sensor was faulty. Such correlation would probably be performed before deciding on a course of action such as plant shutdown.

- *Fault diagnosis.* The next step is to identify the component or components responsible for the problem. Where no further flow readings are available, plant operators might need to go out on the plant and examine runs of pipe work for leakage in order to find out exactly where the problem lies.

- *Repair.* When the fault has been identified, a strategy for curing it can be implemented. If the process plant problem was caused by a pipe leakage, then repair might involve draining off all liquid from the plant, followed by reconstruction work carried out by workers wearing oxygen masks.

2.2.2 Diagnostic Subtasks, Example 2: Car Troubleshooting

The car diagnosis problem, briefly addressed in Chapter 1, can also be broken down into these five subtasks, giving another perspective on how a diagnostic problem can be decomposed:

- *Problem identification.* For a garage-based diagnostic system, problem identification is usually performed by the car driver (perhaps the driver brings the car to the garage complaining that the battery is flat every morning), or by some other system such as an on-board monitoring system (a warning light is illuminated indicating that the battery is not charging).

- *Fault localization.* Given that the problem is with the battery charging/discharging system, then the fault can be restricted to the following causes:
  - problem with the battery charging system;
  - something causing a continual drain on the battery;
  - problem with the battery.

- *Fault identification.* The three possible types of fault can be distinguished by applying a few simple tests to see whether the battery is charging and to see whether the battery holds charge.
- *Fault diagnosis.* If the fault is in the battery charging system, then it can only have been caused by the run of wiring through the alternator to the battery. Probing with a voltage tester should allow identification of point of failure.
- *Repair.* The repair process is fairly trivial in this case, either component replacement or repair of a faulty connection.

2.2.3 Diagnostic Subtasks: Points to Note

- The two examples above illustrate how the importance of each subtask can differ from problem to problem. The main advantage of thinking in terms of these subtasks is that the subtasks provide natural places to decompose a diagnostic system.
- Problem identification only tends to be performed by the diagnostic system when on-line sensor readings are available. Demands for automated problem identification often mean that systems need to consider the kinds of real-time/continuous monitoring issues considered in Chapter 7. Where problem identification is carried out, it can also be used to direct fault localization quite strongly. In other diagnostic systems, the problem identification will already have occurred when the diagnostic system is invoked. A user may have encountered a problem, as is the case with help desk systems, for example, or a separate monitoring system may have detected a problem, and sounded an alarm.
- For the insertion machine example discussed in Section 2.1, the top-level split of the system into smaller fault trees was chosen on the principle of fault localization: the significant symptoms are used to restrict the possible sets of causes for the problem. The problem space is not large enough to need a separate step of fault identification, and so all of the possible causes for a specific set of symptoms are considered in a single small diagnostic fault tree, that is, fault identification and fault diagnosis are lumped together after fault localization has been done. Repair is fairly trivial for the insertion machine, and so is directly attached to the fault diagnosis.
- Fault diagnosis needs to be done to an appropriate level. In an electronic system, there is little point identifying which resistor is broken if the repair action is to replace a board full of resistors and wires. Fault diagnosis should be done to the *least replaceable unit* (LRU). What is regarded as a LRU may change as context changes – perhaps field diagnosis treats a whole circuit board as a LRU, whereas workshop diagnosis of the same circuit board might treat a resistor as a LRU.
- Repair is not always equivalent to component replacement, of course. In the insertion machine example, repair often involves adjustment to the machine to

compensate for wear on the machine or for variations in component dimensions.

2.3 Sources of Diagnostic Material

When building complex diagnostic systems, it is important to make the best possible use of all available information on how to perform diagnosis. Diagnostic system building has often been portrayed as a task to be performed with the close help of an expert. This is not necessarily true. While experience from diagnostic experts is invaluable, most diagnostic situations have a lot of structured information available, and such information can provide a head start in building a diagnostic system. This section identifies the kinds of information that might be available when constructing a diagnostic system.

2.3.1 Existing Diagnostic Information

If examples of the device have been deployed for some time (or where the device is unique, such as a chemical processing plant, if the system itself has been deployed for some time), then there should be records of past problems with the device.

If the device is a consumer product, such as a car or a washing machine, then the most relevant and consistent records are likely to be warranty reports. For diagnosing a manufacturing plant of some kind, the most relevant information will be in engineer logs. In both cases, a warning is in order. Engineers who are troubleshooting a device often do not put record keeping at the top of their list of priorities. Engineers maintaining consumer equipment will often tick the easiest boxes on a form rather than explain a problem in any detail. Manufacturing plant engineers may well only get around to filling in the log at the end of the shift, when some of the details have become hazy.

Even with the above caution, previous diagnostic records can provide two sorts of information:

- *Records of previous problems on the device.* These can contribute to the aim of making sure that the diagnostic system being constructed has reasonable coverage of the system.

- *Component reliability information.* Where a good number of previous failures have occurred, the records can indicate the more likely failures to look for. This information can be very useful for ordering the fault tree.

Where the device to be diagnosed is brand new, useful information can still be gleaned from past records of similar systems. For example, a brand-new car design will be very similar to previous car designs in many ways. It will still use many of the same components, and so previous types of failure will still occur. This means that reused components will probably have similar levels of reliability to the levels experienced in the older designs.

2.3.2 Design Information

The engineers designing a new device will often have produced a report analyzing what kinds of failures can occur on the device. For the automotive and aerospace industries, the relevant reports are the failure mode and effects analysis (FMEA) reports, which consider for each possible component failure what will be the effect on the vehicle as a whole. For the process control industries, the Hazard and Operability (HAZOP) reports will contain relevant information about what kinds of failures can cause specific symptoms to be observed.

In the case of a FMEA report for a device design, it will give a linked set of failure modes with failure effects, also listing the root causes that could make the failure mode happen. For example, in the car electrical circuit mentioned earlier for charging the battery, the failure mode might be "battery not being charged". Effects would be "battery goes flat". Root causes would be "alternator broken", "wire from alternator to battery disconnected", etc.

The failure effects provide details of driver-level symptoms, which will give an idea of the sort of complaint that drivers will have when they return their cars to the garage for mending.

The failure modes provide some fault localization for the user-presented symptoms. They also provide an idea of what sort of coverage of car-level failures needs to be provided by the diagnostic system. Where more than one subsystem in the car can cause the same type of symptom, then further fault localization/fault identification will be needed.

The root causes provide the details for the low-level fault trees performing fault diagnosis.

Where this design information is available, it can provide a good first step towards building a diagnostic system, reducing drastically the amount of valuable time needed from expert diagnosticians in order to build the diagnostic system.

2.4 Design for Diagnosability

Complex electronic systems provide one of the most challenging areas for diagnosis. At the same time, the large number of components involved in an electronic device, even with low component failure rates, means that such systems will frequently have defects at the time of manufacture. It would not be economically feasible to reject all systems with process defects – they need to be repaired so that they can be sold. Because of these factors, the electronics industry is the most advanced in terms of designing devices so that they are as easy as possible to test and repair.

The emphasis of design for testability (DFT) is on manufacturing test, but in practice, design for testability is also design for diagnosability. End-user servicing will usually only replace a whole circuit board, but where a circuit board was designed for easy testability, it is also easy to repair it at a service centre. The same test equipment used to verify that the circuit board was ready for use in the first place can be used to diagnose broken boards.

This section will examine the methods and techniques employed to design circuit boards in such a way that faults are easy to detect and easy to diagnose. Design for testability should be applied at each level in the design of an electronic system (chip, board, system, complete product), but this section will just describe DFT of circuit boards, as that level has the most in common with many of the other devices and systems considered in this book. Finally, the section will also consider to what extent the principles employed when designing circuit boards to be testable can be extended to other kind of devices.

2.4.1 Design for Testability

A common experience in the electronics industry was that designers were making their designs with no reference to how they could be tested or maintained. As circuit boards became more complex, it grew harder and harder to assess whether a manufactured board was fit for purpose or not. In order to test a circuit board, it was necessary to be able to put the board into a desired state, to apply known input data, and to observe outputs to see whether the board operated as expected.

Automated test equipment (ATE) made it simpler to perform a large number of tests on a circuit board, but it was difficult to observe many of the desired values on the board, partly because of the difficulty of finding places to probe on the board, and partly because of the difficulty of setting the board to a state where different parts of the circuitry would be exercised. Observers of the electronics industry talked about an "over the wall" design mentality, where designers designed a new product and then threw it over the wall for other people to worry about how it would be tested and maintained.

Design for testability considers how a particular physical implementation of a logical circuit design will affect the testability of the device. It includes extra work at design time, considering how testable the device is, and how the testability can be improved. It can also mean extra manufacturing expense, if extra logic or extra connections are needed on a circuit board, or extra logic or extra pins on a chip. The extra time needed in the design phase and the extra cost in manufacturing can be justified by greater savings made later on in the lifecycle, because of the high cost of manufacturing test and of maintenance later in the lifecycle.

A number of principles need to be considered and applied during design in order to ensure that a circuit board is testable:

- *Partitioning.* A design can be partitioned in several ways to make it easier to diagnose the component responsible for a problem. First, if a functional group of components can be electrically isolated from the rest of the board, then it can be easier to tell whether that function is working correctly, and to perform fault localization and fault identification. Clustering components by technology, for example, analog and digital components on separate boards where possible, can improve fault diagnosis. Finally, grouping functionally related components physically can make repair easier and reduce the amount of extra on-board circuitry needed for test.

- *Controllability.* The test engineer or automated test equipment (ATE) should be able to initialize the circuit board (or part of the board) to a known state, in order to be able to apply a consistent test. It should then be able to apply a test vector (a known set of inputs) in order to provoke a known output.

- *Observability.* There should be sufficient observation points that inconsistent results to tests can be detected (problem detection), and that sufficient data can be gathered to be able to perform diagnosis to the most accurate level desired – this might be individual component level, but might only be to a group of components.

- *Accessibility.* When designing the board, the designer should bear in mind the type of test equipment to be used, and design appropriately. If a specific type of ATE is being used, that might constrain where components are placed (not too close to the edge of the board, or too near to each other), so that test probes can access the equipment.

For circuit board design, sets of rules have been developed by different researchers to identify when some of these attributes have been infringed by particular physical instantiations of a design. These rules can be applied to identify costly infringements of testability heuristics.

There have also been schemes for ensuring controllability and observability of a device by adding extra circuitry to the board. Boundary scan, for example, is a technique for increasing the testability of a circuit board. There is an IEEE (Institute of Electrical and Electronics Engineers) standard for components to be used in boundary scannable circuits (IEEE Standard 1149.1, IEEE Standard Test Access Port and Boundary Scan Architecture, 1990). It defines that each component meeting the standard should have four additional pins, one each for input and output and two for control. These pins can be used to set the component into testing states, whatever the state of other components linked to the component. Thus, it provides excellent controllability, and can be used to give good partitioning, observability and accessibility. There are a number of standard test features for all components, but the designer can expand the test features of a particular component. Estimates are that it increases the amount of circuitry on a board by between 10 and 25 per cent.

Evaluation of the testability of a circuit board involves simulating possible faults, and seeing to what degree it would be possible to detect and isolate each fault given the design of the circuit board and the testing facilities to be provided. The testability can be expressed as the percentage of total faults that can be uniquely identified.

Testability is a relative measure, and so it is possible to decide which of several physical instantiations of a logical circuit design is most easily testable. That version may not be chosen for implementation, as testability has to be traded against the extra cost of building the more testable circuit. In circuits, if the designer has gone to the trouble of designing a more testable version of the circuit, then it will usually be cost effective, but in other domains, it is less easy to justify the extra expense. Perhaps a better way to approach the problem of testability is to specify testability requirements at the start of design. Design for testability then has several steps:

- *Deciding on the relevant metrics for assessing testability.* Is it necessary to be able to identify single components from test data? Is it sufficient just to be able to blame functional groupings or particular kinds of faults?
- *Identifying the testability features wanted.* Does the board need to fit a particular type of ATE? Is boundary scan testing necessary? Is on-line testing appropriate?
- *Comparing physical designs.* Given clear testability criteria, it is possible to compare the features provided by different solutions, and the cost of those solutions.

Studies indicate that the economics of design for testability are clear. Spending more time on design, and increasing the cost of the device by adding extra circuitry, is generally money well spent if it ensures good testability. The savings in generating tests for the new design, in validating that the design works correctly, in performing manufacturing test and in servicing the boards far outweighs the extra expense incurred.

Given the clear case for employing these design for testability techniques in electronic systems, it is worthwhile to consider why it is so effective in this domain, and why other domains have been slower to adopt such techniques.

2.4.2 Why Does Design for Testability Work so Well for Electronic Devices?

Adding built-in test equipment and ports for automatic test equipment to a device increases the cost of a device. At the same time, it reduces the reliability of the device, because there are more components that can go wrong.

In the electronics field, neither of these effects is particularly serious. The additional wiring increases the cost of the board slightly, and if there are 10 per cent more components, then there is probably a 10 per cent increase in assembly time. However, assembly is automated, and the increase in cost is much less than the cost of the time saved in testing and mending the manufactured components. The reliability of individual components is very high, and the typical environment for the boards is reasonably friendly, and so reliability is not a major issue.

For other domains, the division of costs is very different. Automotive manufacturers are very reluctant to add additional sensors and wires to their vehicles. Cost of components is a much larger issue in this domain. Being able to detect the cause of each failure down to the individual component or wire might increase the cost of a saloon car enough to make it no longer competitive against equivalent models from other manufacturers, and customers do not seem to have diagnosability as a primary criterion when buying a new car. In addition, automobiles are fairly hostile environments for electrical components, and so additional components can affect the reliability of the car significantly. Finally, many non-electrical failures cannot be diagnosed by adding a sensor or two. These facts mean that in order to diagnose some failures on cars, tests will need to be performed by engineers. This means that the notion of testability given for electronic devices is too simplistic.

In the first place, we assumed for electronic devices that all failures were equally likely. That is certainly not the case with cars or planes. Using information about mean time between failures (MTBF), a group from Oregon State University working with Boeing (Clark and Paasch, 1996) has proposed a set of metrics for deciding on the diagnosability of a device which takes into account the likelihood of each failure as well as the ability to distinguish between failures. It was also assumed that the cost of testing was constant for electronic components. This is not the case for many kinds of device, and so cost of testing also needs to be included in a diagnosability measure for devices where there are significant differences between the costs of different tests. Nevertheless, a measure for diagnosability that included all of these factors could lead to useful improvements in designers' appreciation of diagnosability issues.

Chemical process plants tend to have an increasing amount of instrumentation, providing the kind of observability that one would desire. This domain is also fairly hostile to sensors, but the lack of reliability can be overcome by providing analytical redundancy – comparing readings over time can help decide whether there is a problem with a process or whether a sensor has failed. In general though, it is not possible to initialize the state of part of the chemical plant independently from the rest, and so tests cannot be carried out on one isolated part of the plant.

Designers need to identify states in which diagnosis can be carried out and measure the cost of extra sensors against diagnosability and against the need for analytical redundancy.

2.4.3 What General Principles of Diagnosability Can be Extracted?

At the outset of the design process, the designer should decide on the level of diagnosability that is desired.

- What are the least replaceable components?
- Should the device be able to distinguish between all possible failures automatically?

- Should it be able to tell the difference between important failures (e.g. for a car, failures which would cause the vehicle to become unsafe) and unimportant failures?

Fault simulation at design time enables identification of possible diagnostic problems. This is important assistance for designers to understand the ramifications of their design. In some domains, such simulation can be automated (see Section 6.2 for an example of this), but in others it will need to be performed in the engineer's head. Either way, diagnosability of a design can be measured from the degree to which different failures can be distinguished. Such measures may need to take into account the reliability of different types of component, and the cost of different kinds of tests.

Where there are choices between designs and all other things are equal, then the design that provides improved diagnosability should be chosen. Where other matters (cost, reliability, aesthetic appeal) are not equal, then the designer will have to trade these characteristics against diagnosability to reach an acceptable design solution.

3. Tools for Complex Fault Trees

When the examples of diagnostic systems given in Chapters 1 and 2 were developed, they were first drawn on paper as diagnostic fault trees and then implemented in an expert systems language. The implementation phase can be lengthy, and gives the possibility of introducing errors when converting the design for the diagnostic system into a computer program.

The implementation phase of the diagnostic system development process can be done automatically, by using tools that enable the developer to build a diagnostic fault tree graphically. The tool will then generate a computer program from the graphical fault tree. This avoids the possibility of user-introduced programming errors. A second advantage of this approach is that the engineers using the diagnostic tool will understand the graphical fault tree representation, and may be willing to maintain the graphical representation (and thus the diagnostic system) themselves.

This chapter has examples of three tools for generating diagnostic systems from graphical fault trees:

- GRAF2. This is a simple public domain tool for illustrating the idea of generating diagnostic systems from fault trees.

- TestBench™ from Carnegie Group. This is a general commercial tool for building diagnostic systems from fault trees.

- GRADE™ from GenRad. This is a more targeted tool than TestBench, with extra facilities specific to the construction of diagnostic applications for electrical systems.

3.1 Graphical Fault Tree Building: A Simple Example

This section gives an example of a simple graphical diagnostic system builder, GRAF2. It illustrates the principle of how a graphical tool can be used to generate a diagnostic system, and, unlike the commercial tools described later in the chapter, it is freely available via the Web for readers to experiment with at their leisure.

The motivation behind the GRAF2 tool was a particular diagnostic problem that highlights the kind of application for which this type of graphic-based tool is ideal.

An elevator manufacturer was interested in a knowledge-based system for field use by maintenance engineers. The number of maintenance engineers was large, and so to minimize cost, such a system would need to run on cheap palm-top computers such as the pocket-sized 3Com PalmPilot or the compact Psion 5.

After each repair, maintenance engineers had to fill out a diagnostic report, with the result that many examples of solutions to past problems were available. However, case-based reasoning (see Chapter 4) was not very appropriate. Available cases contained details of the symptoms and the associated remedies, but did not contain information about the most efficient order in which to carry out tests on the elevator system.

In elevator maintenance, correct ordering of tests is vital in order to achieve efficient diagnosis. Imagine what might happen if the engineer adopted the simple strategy of performing the test for the most likely diagnosis at each point in the investigation. The order of investigation might look like this:

> Go to the basement and test resistor R3 in the control system.
> Go to floor 7 and test "elevator on this floor" detector.
> Go to floor 1 and test "elevator on this floor" detector.
> Go to roof space and test the end-stop detector.

This scenario appears even worse when you recall that the elevator is not working! Because of the comparative cost of performing different tests at a particular point in the diagnostic investigation, an efficient fault tree is extremely important in this domain. A case-based system that suggested past cases, but did not order them efficiently, would not be useful in this domain. On the other hand, it would be equally foolish to carry out all possible tests in the basement if some of those tests took half an hour to complete and were extremely unlikely. It is necessary to have a diagnostic strategy that balances the different diagnostic costs.

As the elevator maintenance engineers are the experts on efficient diagnosis, this application demands that it should be possible to present them with fault trees that they can understand, discuss together and modify. A second vital requirement is that the diagnostic system should be available on site wherever an elevator is being mended, and so any host computer would need to be very light. A graphical fault tree builder that is able to generate executable code that can be run on a small hand-held computer is a good solution for this application.

While the elevator application provided the motivation for building GRAF2, the use of GRAF2 will be illustrated by a more familiar example – the car diagnostic example presented in Chapter 1.

The GRAF2 screen shown in Figure 3.1 allows the user to choose to add either question nodes or advice nodes to the fault tree. For either kind of node, the user is prompted for some text to be inserted in the node. If the node is a question node, then the text should be the question text or the details of the test to be performed. If the node is an advice node, then the text should be the advice to be given if that node is reached. Nodes can be connected by clicking in a connector box on the "from" node and then clicking in the "to" node. Question nodes have two connector boxes (one for the "Yes" answer and one for the "No" answer).

Advice nodes also have a connector box, allowing intermediate advice to be given during the diagnostic consultation, and then further questions to be asked.

Construction in GRAF2 of the fault tree first shown in Figure 1.1 is illustrated in Figure 3.1, with further parts of the fault tree being accessible by scrolling the window.

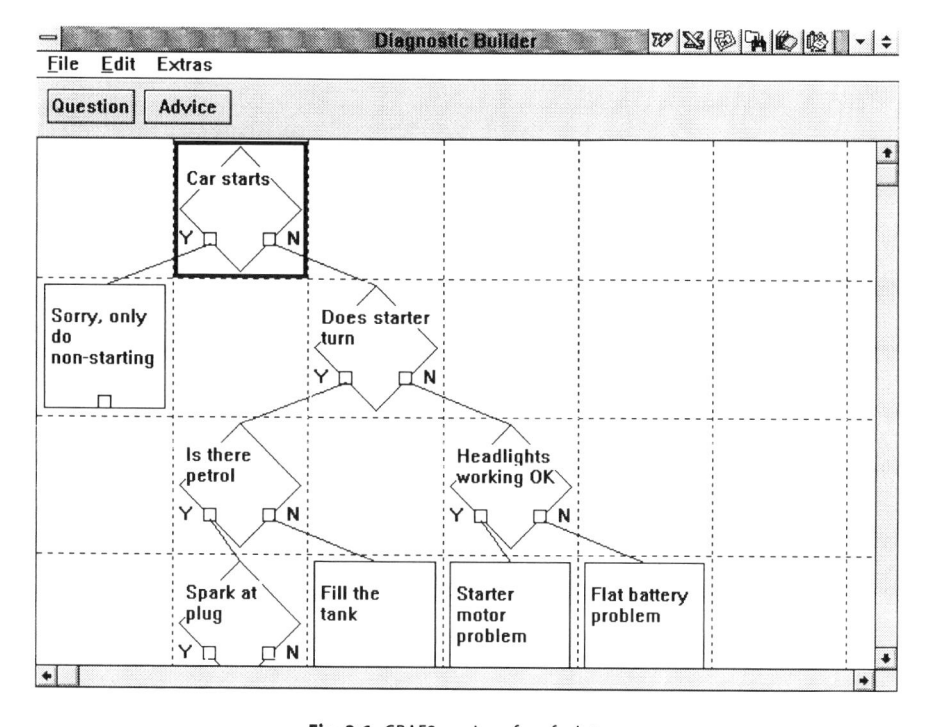

Fig. 3.1 GRAF2 version of car fault tree.

When the graphical representation of the tree has been input, it can be printed out and discussed by the engineers. Once they are agreed that it is a reasonable representation of the way to approach the diagnostic problem, then runnable programs can be generated by GRAF2. It can generate code for Turbo Pascal, ANSI standard C, or for downloading to a PalmPilot.

The PalmPilot version would be particularly appropriate for the elevator diagnosis application briefly discussed at the start of this chapter. The cost of providing laptop computers to all of the elevator engineers prohibits that from being a practical solution. In any case, carrying a laptop PC around a building while performing diagnosis would not be a popular idea.

A palmtop computer such as the PalmPilot, executing code generated by a graphically-based diagnostic constructor such as GRAF2, would be an excellent solution to many field diagnosis problems. The cost of a PalmPilot is an order of magnitude less than the cost of a laptop PC, and so could easily be cost-justified by the savings in diagnostic time. The weight of the PalmPilot would be negligible compared with the toolkit needed to fix any problems. However, for maximum benefit, you would want to integrate the diagnostic system with other engineer support systems such as the ability to download or upload customer visit reports and supplementary information about the devices being diagnosed. Estimates of the savings available by providing such support to a diagnostic engineer vary from half an hour to two hours per engineer per day.

Examples of the code generated and of the execution of this example application are provided in Appendix 2. The code generated is the minimum necessary for generating a fault tree, but it would be possible to improve GRAF2 to allow the user to add other attributes to each node of the tree, such as:

- Further information for the user about how to perform a test, as is available in the Adviser code shown earlier.

- Graphical illustration. It would be possible to link a picture to each node, so that the user could see a picture of the test or repair to be done.

- The ability to retract answers to questions and so move back up the diagnostic fault tree.

It would also be possible to improve the GRAF2 tree building options:

- Better types of node. GRAF2 would benefit from having multiple choice nodes to compact the tree.

- More modularity. It would be useful to be able to define a fault subtree, and then refer to that subtree from different points in a higher level tree.

- Good examination and printing facilities for large trees. A useful feature in a commercial graphical tree builder is to be able to show trees at different levels of resolution on the screen, and print them off as a large tree.

The usefulness of the GRAF2 system can be illustrated by the fact that it has been employed on a variety of diagnostic system building projects. For several of those projects it was necessary to generate non-Pascal code, and so two other code-generation systems have been built for GRAF2, one to generate Adviser code, and one to generate COGSYS rules. Drawing the fault tree in GRAF2 has twin benefits over directly coding a diagnostic system: it documents the structure of the diagnostic system and makes it available to engineers in a form which they can understand; it also generates runnable code much faster than it can be written by a programmer and makes it more maintainable. GRAF2 can be downloaded from the Web site supporting this book.

Although GRAF2 is useful, it is a long way from being a commercial tool for building large diagnostic systems, as can be inferred from the limitations discussed above. The rest of this chapter describes two commercial diagnostic tree-building systems that are much more developed and provide some of the levels of support missing in GRAF2.

3.2 TestBench

TestBench™ is a commercial tool from Carnegie Group for constructing and deploying diagnostic applications. It runs on PCs and is made up of three parts:

- TestBuilder™. This is a graphical tree builder providing a more sophisticated version of the features seen in the simple GRAF2 example.
- TestBridge™. This tool translates the graphical tree into a diagnostic system which can be executed by TestView.
- TestView. This is the user interface to the diagnostic system. It executes the produced diagnostic system.

This section will look at the three components of the TestBench system, and then give an example of how TestBench has been used.

3.2.1 TestBuilder

TestBuilder is the graphical front end of TestBench for building the diagnostic tree. The GRAF2 diagnostic system builder gives the basic idea of what is involved in using a system such as TestBuilder. TestBuilder has more features than the simple GRAF2 system, and different sorts of nodes for building the tree, but the user is still building a diagnostic fault tree by placing nodes in a window and linking them together.

Instead of nodes in the tree containing a two-way test, where you branch left if the answer is "Yes" and right if the answer is "No", a single node can be linked to a number of related tests. This makes the tree somewhat more compressed, and therefore easier to comprehend as the tree grows larger, because you can see more of the tree at once.

Figure 3.2 shows the arrangement of the tree. It is displayed in a format very similar to the display of the Windows file and directory tree. Nodes which are not leaf nodes can be either displayed as expanded (shown as boxes containing a "–") or not expanded (shown as boxes containing a "+").

The top levels of the hierarchy shown in Figure 3.2 are *categories*, and are used for problem identification (as discussed in Chapter 2), enabling the user of the system to focus in on the particular kind of problem. Below that, the nodes with names beginning with "S", for example "S-NOT-BOOTING-FROM-FLOPPY" are *symptoms*, used for performing fault localization/fault identification.

At the bottom level, the nodes with names beginning with "F" are failures: the actual problems that could cause the higher level symptoms. This information is used to perform fault diagnosis and repair (using the terms discussed in Chapter 2). At this level, the tree contains ordering information: nodes at one level of the hierarchy shown higher up the screen will be investigated before nodes lower down the screen; so in Figure 3.2, failure F-NOT-A-BOOTABLE-FLOPPY will be investigated before F-FLOPPY-DRIVE-NOT-DEFINED-IN-SYSTEM. This allows the system builder to dictate the order in which the tests should be carried out.

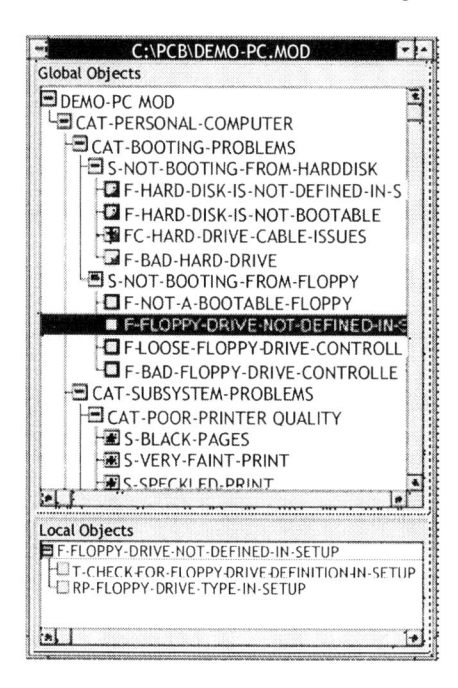

Fig. 3.2 Display of fault tree in TestBuilder.

Each failure node can contain, or point to, a great deal of information designed to make diagnosis more efficient and effective:

- *Description.* A short textual description of the problem, used at run-time to browse the fault tree.

- *Detailed description.* This is used to allow the user to type in a description of the problem and look for matching nodes rather than browsing to find the fault.

- *Browsing enabled.* This flag indicates whether the user can browse this part of the fault tree.

- *Tests.* Diverse information about testing can be included here. Tests to be carried out can be attached to a failure node. Such tests can include instructions/diagrams for carrying out the test. Tests can be grouped into families so that related tests will be performed together in order to improve efficiency.

- *Repairs.* Repair nodes give details of how to remedy the failure identified by the tests.

- *Rules.* These allow run-time alteration of the fault tree. For example, the system might reorder the investigation of fault nodes if it is informed that the device being diagnosed is from a particular model year where different failures than normal were prevalent. Figure 3.3 shows an example of the information for one of the failure nodes in the tree in Figure 3.2.

3.2.2 TestBridge

The TestBridge tool takes the diagnostic tree built with the help of the TestBuilder tool, and turns it into code that can be executed in the TestView system. This tool hardly seems worth naming – it is the equivalent of a "Save as" option in a word processing program.

3.2.3 TestView

TestView is the user interface to the executable system. It interprets the knowledge base and presents the result to the end user. A version of it exists within TestBuilder, so that the developer of the diagnostic system can test the system as it will appear to the user. The stand-alone version delivered to the end user only allows execution of the diagnostic system, not editing of the knowledge base.

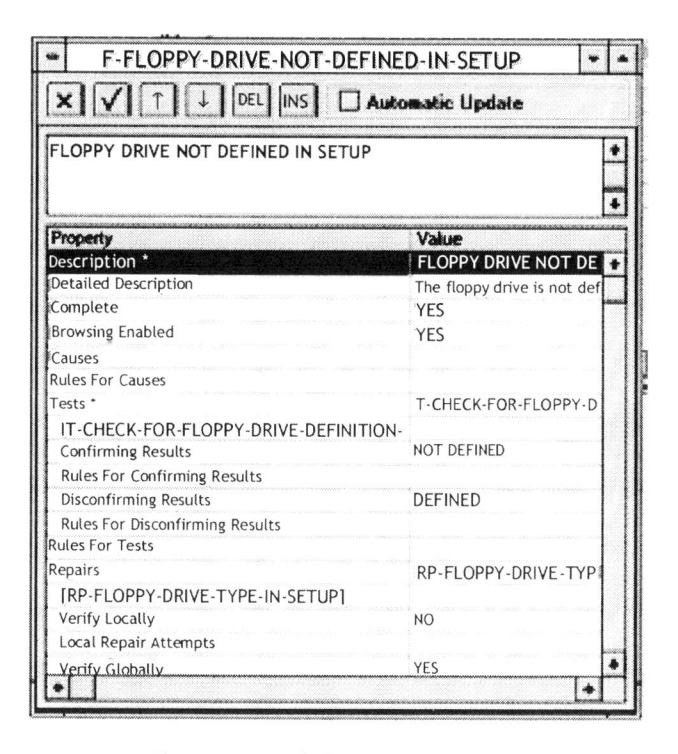

Fig. 3.3 Details of a fault node in TestBuilder.

The produced diagnostic system can be presented to the user in different ways. This is very sensible, as it takes into account the different levels of experience of users and the different amount of knowledge that might be held about a problem. The simplest version of the TestView interface asks questions of the user in the same way that GRAF2 does. Figure 3.4 shows an example of this, where the user is asked to carry out a test, and can choose an item from the menu to signal the result of the test. The next test or diagnosis will depend on the reply given to the test.

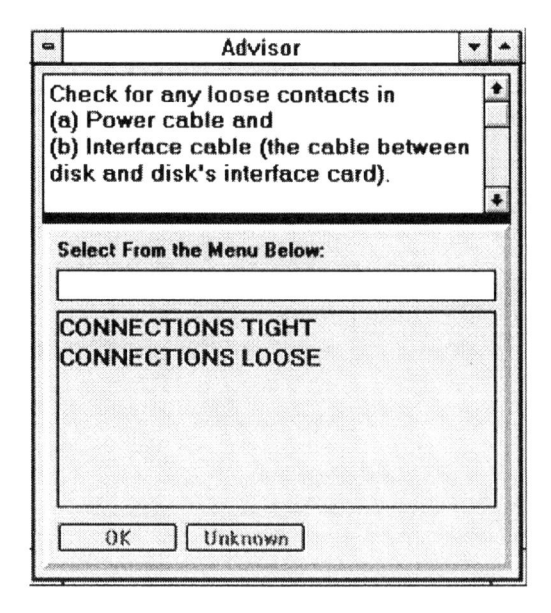

Fig. 3.4 TestView fault test information.

A different strategy can be employed with more sophisticated users. TestView can present the user with a Fault Browser, as illustrated in Figure 3.5. The fault browser allows the user to take a number of different actions depending on what they know about the diagnostic situation.

- *Describe.* The user can type in a description of the situation. It will be matched against different leaf failure nodes, and an ordered list of nodes that match the description will be displayed to the user (best matching cases at the top of the list).

- *Focus.* The user can navigate through the tree of categories and symptoms until a set of leaf nodes is reached. This allows quick focusing where the fault has already been localized.

- *Tests.* The present set of possible diagnoses is displayed in the browser. The user can select one and choose to perform tests to verify whether it is the actual failure.

- *Repairs.* Once the failure has been identified through testing, or if the user already knew the failure when starting TestView, the user can be given instructions on how to fix the problem.

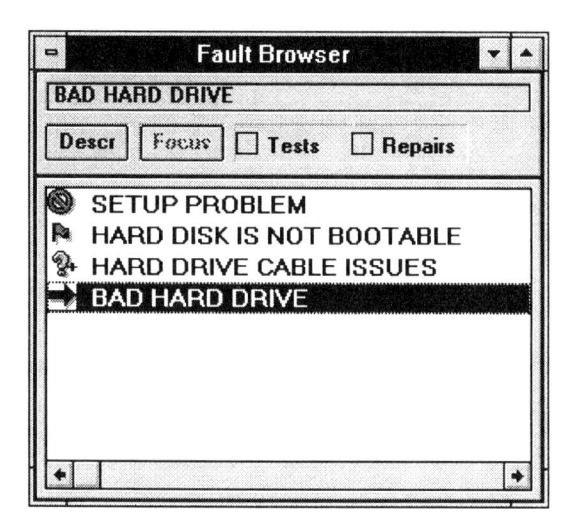

Fig. 3.5 TestView Fault Browser.

3.2.4 Example Application of TestBench

Picker International, a billion pound turnover supplier of medical diagnostic systems, used TestBench to implement Questor, a system providing support to their field engineers diagnosing and repairing their products.

The field engineers were already supplied with laptops for other purposes, and so existing hardware could be used to provide on-line help to engineers at minimum extra cost.

The Questor system uses the features of TestBench described in this chapter. These features enable the provision of a standardized diagnostic approach that has been refined by Picker diagnostic experts over the years. It is implemented as a diagnostic tree, as outlined above. The branches of the diagnostic tree are annotated with "why" information that explain the purpose of the proposed test, as well as "how" information about how to carry out the tests.

When the Questor system is run by the field engineer, it includes a notepad for field engineers to record possible improvements to or errors in Questor. The notepad details and a log of the diagnostic pathway traversed during the diagnosis can be transmitted to central support if any updates to Questor are needed. This link provides feedback for improvement of the Questor system.

3.3 GRADE™

The GRADE™ diagnostic authoring toolset from GenRad is a good example of a diagnostic system-building toolset designed for a specific area of application.

GRADE has been designed for the purpose of building diagnostic applications for the electrical systems for automobiles, and GenRad claim that using GRADE is at least five times as efficient as writing code.

GRADE enables the construction of the type of fault tree already seen in the other examples in this chapter, and also has several very valuable extra features that are specific to the types of applications for which it is intended. While it was originally applied in the automobile industry, it is more generally applicable and would prove useful for building any diagnostic systems that needed to interface with complex electrical and electromechanical equipment.

3.3.1 Overview

This section will look at the features of GRADE in some detail, but here is a brief summary of the most important points:

- *Fault tree design facilities.* GRADE provides the ability to build the types of fault tree that have already been discussed in this chapter, with some extra features specific to electrical system diagnosis.

- *Separate specification of graphic and textual details.* Pictures and text need to be changed more often than the basic structure of the fault tree, and so they are defined as separate items that are referenced from the tree. This can give some software engineering advantages.

- *Generation of code.* GRADE can generate a single executable program from the fault tree, graphics and text.

- *Good testing facilities.* GRADE can emulate the run-time environment of the diagnostic system on a normal PC, and provides facilities to follow the execution of the fault tree.

- *Runnable on diagnostic test equipment.* The program generated by GRADE can also be executed on GenRad's GDS3000 series diagnostic computers in use by technicians in automobile workshops.

In order to understand some of the features of GRADE, it is beneficial to understand the context in which the diagnostic systems built with GRADE are used. Car electrical systems have gradually become more complex. As that has happened, misdiagnosis of problems has increased, and many automobile manufacturers have begun to respond to that increase.

One response is to build more monitoring systems into cars, so that the monitoring systems detect and record problems in the form of diagnostic trouble codes (DTCs). This is termed *on-board* detection of faults. On-board detection can usually only detect problems and decide on a course of action. Problems can either be severe enough to mean that the car should be stopped immediately, or can allow "limp home" functionality, where the driver is warned of the problem and is informed that the car should be serviced as soon as possible, but that the problem is not severe enough to prevent the operation of the car in the short term.

A second response is to provide automated diagnostic assistance in automobile service centres. The assistance usually takes the form of a computer running a diagnostic program, often with access to other useful information such as on-line manuals. The service centre diagnostic computer will be linked to the car in order to read DTCs from the on-board diagnostic system, and will have other sensors that the technicians can link to the car so that instrument test readings can be read directly by the diagnostic system rather than entered on the keyboard by the technician.

GRADE provides facilities for constructing diagnostic programs for use by technicians in automobile service centres. Figure 3.6 shows the context in which such diagnostic programs operate. The technician can talk to the driver to obtain the symptoms that caused the driver to bring in the car in the first place. The technician can use these symptoms to guide the investigation carried out by the diagnostic program.

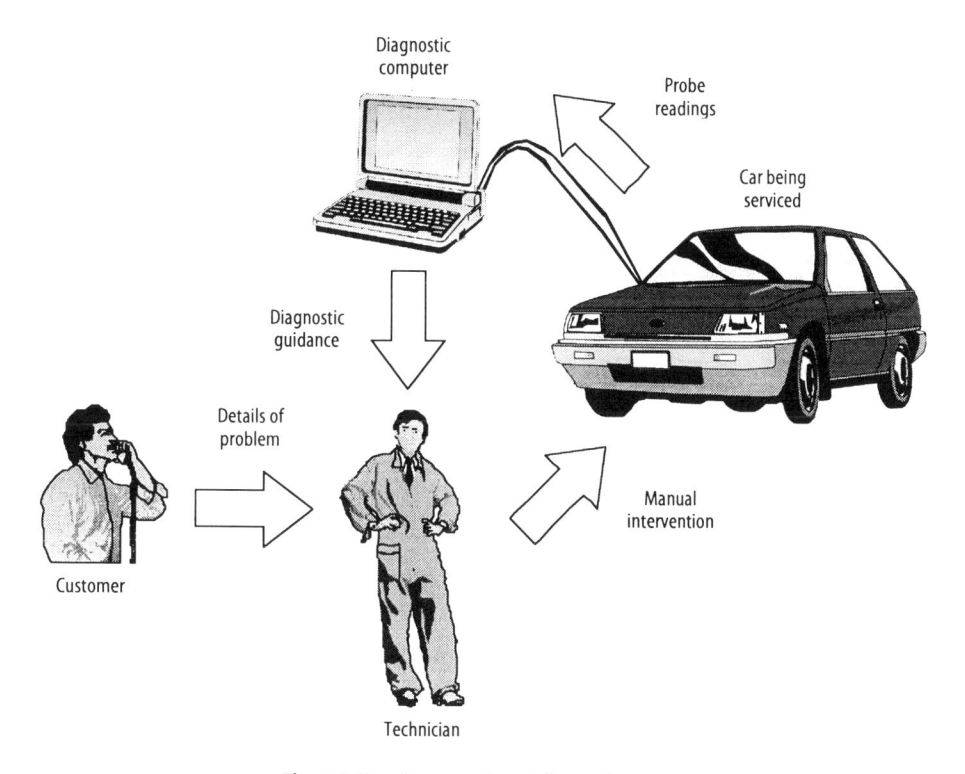

Fig. 3.6 Use of a garage-based diagnostic system.

The diagnostic symptom is linked to the car, and can also use diagnostic trouble codes as starting points for diagnosis. During the investigation, the diagnostic system will keep the technician informed of the likely failures and will request tests to be performed. These might entail the technician setting the car into a particular state, for example running the engine until normal operating temperature is reached, or might entail performing tests. Some tests will be carried out by the technician, others will involve the technician in connecting probes from the diagnostic system to the car so that the diagnostic system can read test values directly from the car's on-board electronics.

When a diagnosis has been made, the diagnostic system will provide the technician with repair information. Further tests might need to be performed in order to verify that the repair was successful, and the diagnostic system will be able to guide the technician through those tests as well.

The rest of this section will describe the representational features of GRADE, and then explain how GRADE can help the diagnostic system builder through the process of using GRADE to build and test an automotive diagnostic system. The simple car diagnostic system developed in earlier chapters will be used as a basis for this, and extended to add a test interface to the vehicle to check voltage.

3.3.2 Representational Features of GRADE

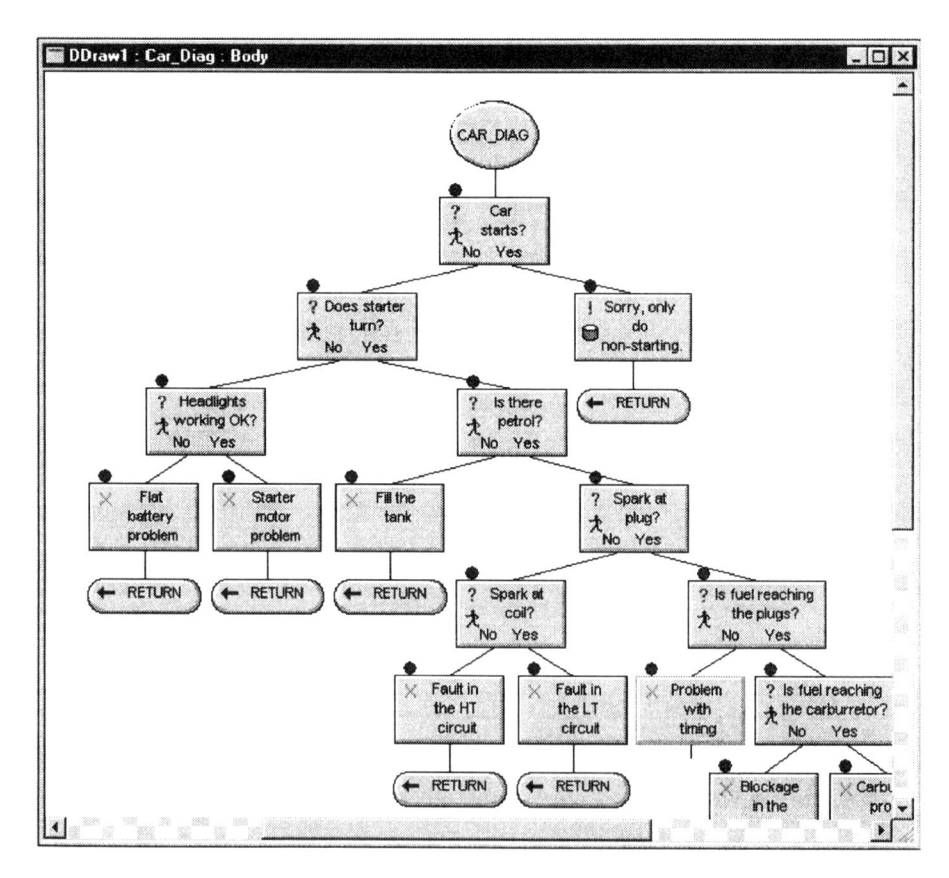

Fig. 3.7 Simple car diagnosis system in GRADE.

Tools for Complex Fault Trees

The basis of GRADE is the same kind of fault tree that has already been illustrated several times. Figure 3.7 shows a GRADE version of the fault tree for car diagnosis introduced in Chapter 1. The symbols in the fault tree have the following meanings:

!   This is an action to be taken. In the example above, the only action is to give some advice.

?   This is a test to be done. Like the previous systems, it can have a Yes or No answer. The picture of a person on the tests means that it is a test to be done by the technician. A picture of a car would mean that it was an automated test.

X   This symbol signifies a diagnosis has been made.

←   This symbol followed by the word RETURN signifies the end of that line of reasoning.

The contents of a node in the tree are added in a similar dialog to the previous systems discussed in this chapter. Figure 3.8 shows the details of one of the operator questions being entered. As well as the text of the question, the node can be annotated with comments explaining why the question is being asked, and with program code. When the fault tree is turned into program code, any code specified here will be added to the program.

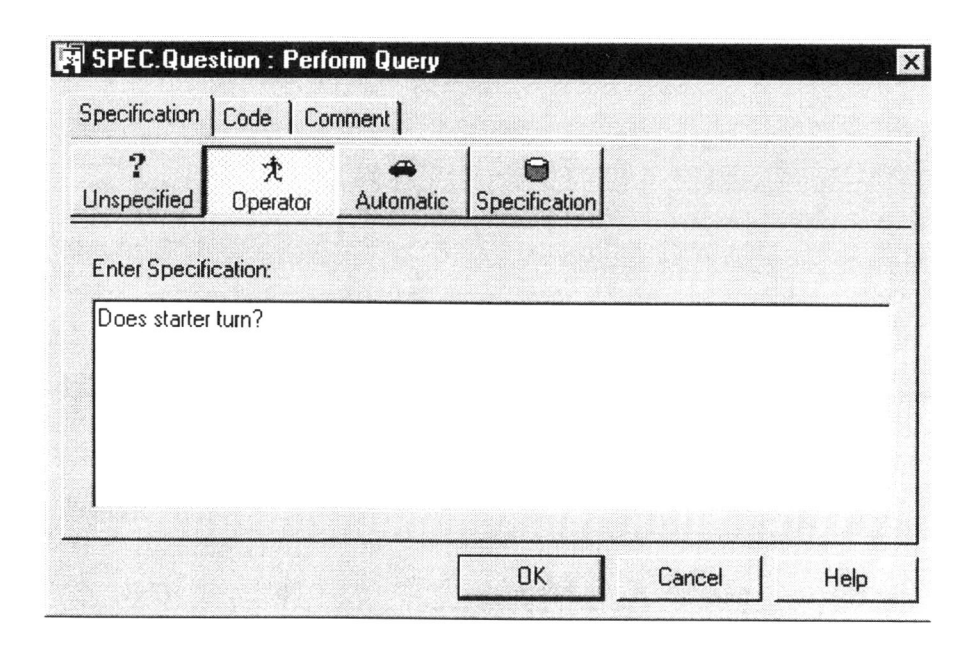

Fig. 3.8 Question node details in GRADE.

The simple example diagnostic system does not include some of the features of GRADE that make it most useful for building complex systems in its application area. Two examples of these features are shown in Figure 3.9. They are the ability to interface directly to the car, and the ability to break large fault trees down into linked simpler fault trees.

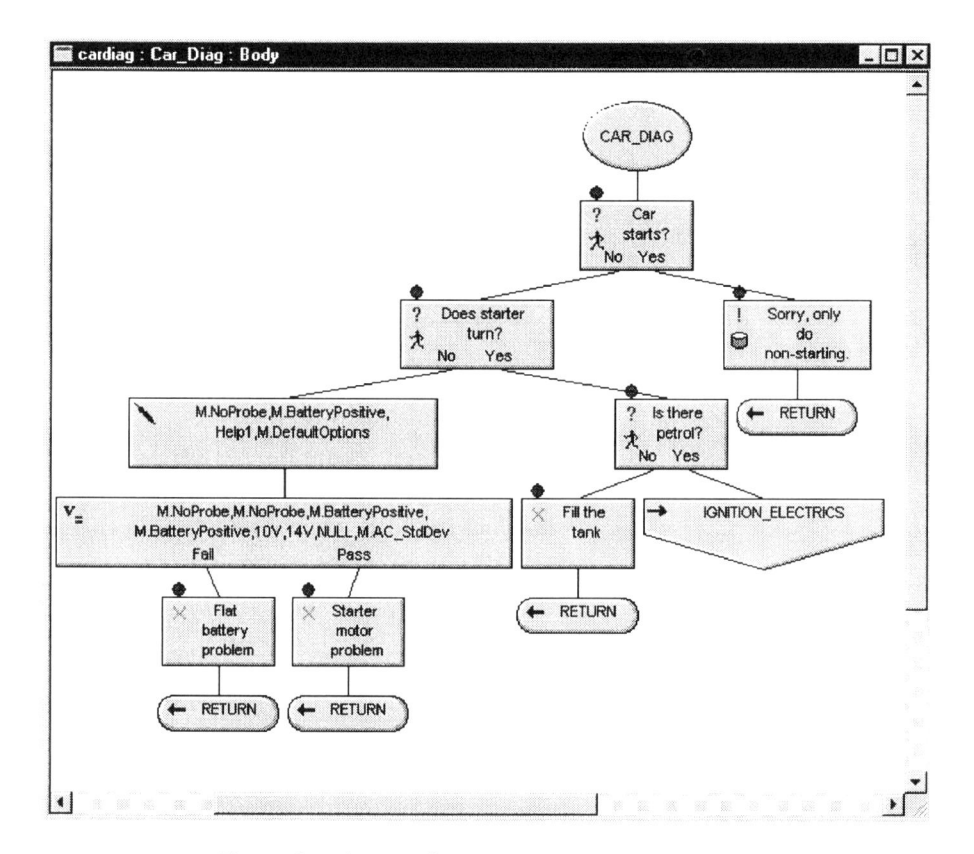

Fig. 3.9 Second version of simple car diagnostic system in GRADE.

The question "Headlights OK?" on the left of the original fault tree has been replaced by two nodes. The first added node, with the ⬉ symbol on it, is a node that prompts the technician to place a probe on the positive terminal of the battery. The second node, with the $V_=$ symbol, generates program code to read the voltage value at the probe, and check whether it is within normal operating range for the battery. Each of these functions is fairly complex, as can be seen at a glance, but the graphical fault tree building interface makes it as easy as possible to fill in values, prompting the user to choose from the legal values for parameters such as probe names, and suggesting default values for many parameters.

GRADE has libraries of further functions to deal with different types of interface. These can range from simple extensions such as multiple choice questions, through interface routines that can read values from test probes, to complex database access routines.

Tools for Complex Fault Trees

The second major improvement in this version of the diagnostic tree is that a major part of the tree has been collapsed into a subtree. All of the questions concerned with the ignition electrical system have been collapsed into an IGNITION_ELECTRICS subtree. Double clicking on the IGNITION_ELECTRICS subtree symbol would bring up the window shown in Figure 3.10. This could then be edited separately from the main tree. Such a subtree can be linked to several other parts of the main tree, giving the ability to modularise the tree in a sensible way. It also means that the whole tree can be shown as an overview, and details are available to be examined where necessary.

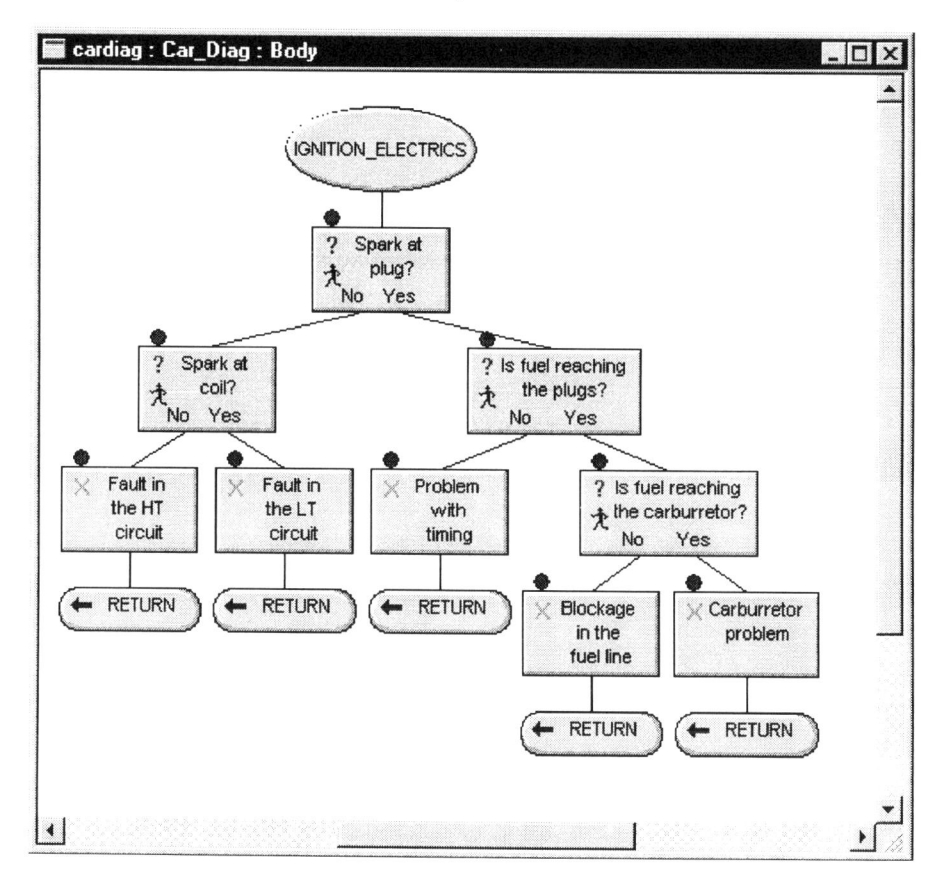

Fig. 3.10 Subtree for second version of car diagnostic system.

GRADE provides tree-checking facilities. If there are unattached nodes in the tree, or if a parameter has been filled in with an illegal value, then GRADE will refuse to compile the tree and will flag the node or nodes causing the problem. This can save the developer a lot of time in testing and debugging. When the tree is legal, the developer can choose to generate PAL2 code from it. PAL2 is an interpreted language run on GenRad's target diagnostic systems.

The automobile diagnostic systems built with GRADE need to be localized for different countries around the world, so another useful feature is the ability to define all text separately from the structure of the diagnostic system. This makes it much easier to maintain the resulting diagnostic systems. The diagnostic systems can be internationalized by replacing a text file, and the structure can be altered in a single version without necessarily having to update all of the different language versions.

3.3.3 Testing a GRADE Application

GRADE provides good support for the process of testing the constructed diagnostic system. The eventual intention is that the diagnostic system should run on GenRad's diagnostic hardware, linked to the car being serviced. However, it is tedious to download it to the actual target hardware in order to test that the diagnostic strategy is correct.

For this reason, GRADE provides emulation facilities for the target hardware on ordinary development PCs. There are two parts to this emulation. GRADE emulates the screen presentation of the target system, presenting screens that appear as they will in the final diagnostic system. It also provides emulation for the hardware interfaces to the car, so that the developer can test the diagnostic system's response to different instrument readings on the car.

Figure 3.11 shows an example screen from the emulator. It displays one of the questions from the simple car diagnostic system. Note the large icons from the target system, making it easy for the technician to respond to the screen in a difficult environment.

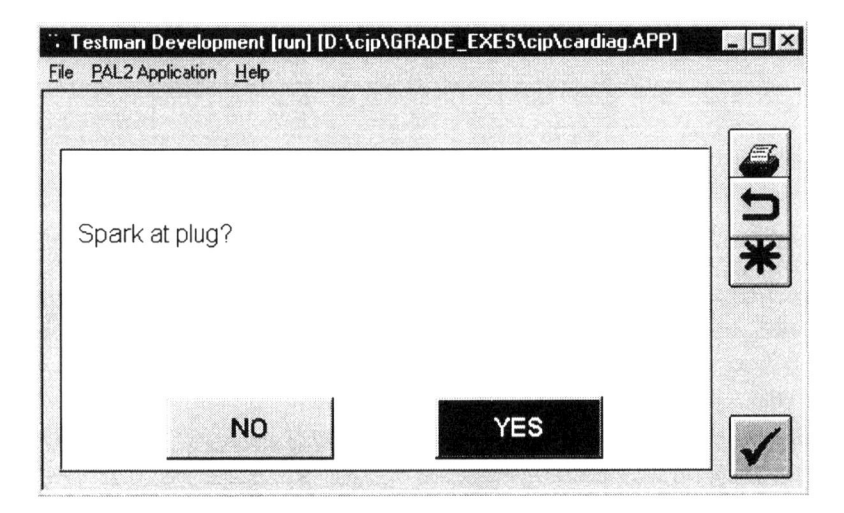

Fig. 3.11 Test run of diagnostic system.

The buttons on the right of the emulator screen provide the following extra features:

Tools for Complex Fault Trees

🖨	The technician can print out the screen contents. This is extremely useful when the screen contains detailed instructions or a diagram of what needs to be done.
↩	The technician can use this button to move back up the fault tree, and re-answer questions differently.
✻	This button allows the technician to interrupt the running of the diagnostic system and start again.

The engineer can obtain a good impression of what the diagnostic system will look like on the target system by running the system under emulation on the development PC, using this interface.

The diagnostic system will contain instructions to the technician to connect probes to the car, and routines to read and act on the values at the probes. In order to be able to emulate this on a development PC, GRADE replaces any calls to the probe reading interface, passing them to a measurement emulation tool, as illustrated in Figure 3.12.

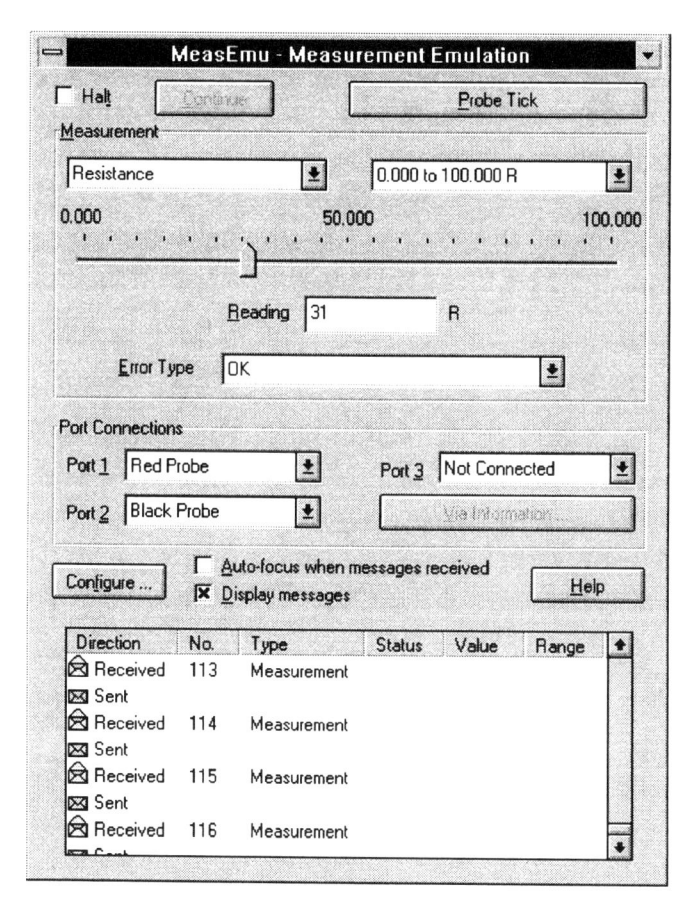

Fig. 3.12 Measurement emulation interface screen.

The measurement emulation tool displays the name of the probe reading that would be requested from the car, and allows the developer to set the value of the simulated reading. This is much better than just providing a default value from an interface stub routine, as it allows the developer to test the effect of different values being input to the diagnostic system.

GRADE also contains routines to interface to the on-board diagnostic computers in the car. Emulation of the interface to on-board hardware is provided by another tool similar to the measurement emulation tool, allowing the specification of a series of information to be read as values from the on-board computer.

When building a diagnostic system for a whole car, the lower levels of the system are constructed as illustrated in this section, with fault identification, fault diagnosis and repair encapsulated in trees. Fault localization would be tedious to perform through the type of single choice question shown here, and there are two sensible possibilities depending on the level of technology available on the car.

For cars with advanced on-board diagnostic systems, it is possible to read diagnostic trouble codes directly from the car. They will narrow down the diagnosis to a single lower level tree. With less advanced cars, series of menus are used to enable the technician to select the subsystem(s) that might be at fault.

3.4 Summary and Conclusions

The approach described in this chapter works for complex practical diagnostic applications. Companies are using this approach to build large applications such as whole car diagnostic systems.

Tools such as GRADE provide many extra features that simplify the fault tree building process:

- more complex structures (different question types, subtrees, reuse of subtrees, return values etc);
- better interfaces (reading probe values, interfacing to on-board computers);
- emulation of target hardware.

Provision of such facilities means that professional fault tree building tools are among the best solutions for diagnostic system building for applications such as car diagnostics where large integrated diagnostic systems with a clear strategy need to be built.

4. *Case-Based Diagnostic Systems*

4.1 What is Case-Based Reasoning?

Case-based reasoning (CBR) is a way of using past solutions to a particular kind of problem to solve similar new problems (Kolodner, 1993; Watson, 1997). CBR has been enjoying considerable attention over the past few years – the subjects offered as tutorials at major artificial intelligence and expert systems conferences indicate what aspects of knowledge-based systems are thought to be most relevant to the attendees, and tutorials on CBR have been on constant offer for several years.

CBR may be considered as being analogous to human experts solving a problem by employing their relevant past experience as far as possible. If the new problem has some novel aspects, then the solution to the new problem is added to their expertise. It is particularly suited to application areas where the problems may not be decomposed easily or where the general principles involved are not well understood, but where there is a library of past experience that can be employed.

CBR is presented in the research literature (Hammond, 1989; Kolodner, 1993) as working in the following way:

- Select a suitable case from a case-base of past solutions to problems, by matching a description of the new problem that needs to be solved with the stored descriptions of already solved problems.

- Adapt the solution used by the selected past case to suit the requirements of the current situation.

- Produce a new solution and evaluate it.

- If it is a good solution, store the description of the new problem just solved, together with the new solution, as a case in the case-base.

CBR is applicable to many types of problem-solving, but has proven extremely popular in the area of diagnosis, especially as technical support for help desk applications. The general characteristics of successful case-based diagnostic systems are:

- *Broad but shallow domain.* This was expressed earlier in the book as "the diagnostic problem is not a single tree, but a forest of small trees". There are a number of loosely connected problems that must be dealt with, and they need different kinds of expertise. This can be contrasted with the elevator diagnosis problem discussed in Chapter 3, where the investigation of the different possibilities is strongly linked.

- *Experience, rather than theory, is the primary source of knowledge.* In order to diagnose effectively in the domain, it is necessary to have seen many past examples of problems that occur, rather than having a deep understanding of the domain.

- *Solutions are reusable.* When a new problem is seen, it is likely that it can be solved using an old solution. If each problem is different, then there is little to be gained by trying to reuse past solutions.

When CBR is used for practical diagnostic systems, it can be portrayed as performing a more specific set of actions than the general CBR methodology described at the start of this chapter. A more precise description of case-based reasoning for device diagnosis might be:

- Obtain symptoms of the new diagnostic problem (from the user or from another system).

- Match the symptoms with the descriptions of previous problems (often referred to as cases), retrieving previous problems with similar symptoms.

- Perform tests to distinguish between the previous problems that match the symptoms. This might be done by investigating the best matching case first, or by ordering the matching cases by frequency of occurrence. In order to accomplish this task, some information about how to perform fault localization and/or fault diagnosis (see Section 2.2 for definitions of these terms) needs to be added to the case-base or to the diagnostic system.

- If the new problem was different from any previously known problem, it should be added to the case-base. In practical diagnostic systems, this is usually not done automatically. Adding cases is more likely to be done during a maintenance phase, where an expert verifies the cases before they are added to the case-base.

Figure 4.1 illustrates the diagnostic case-based reasoning process described above. In order to build such a diagnostic system, there are several questions that need to be addressed:

- What kinds of past cases exist?
- How should a case be represented?
- How should the symptoms be matched to past cases?
- How can the matched cases be ranked for investigation?
- How do you verify whether a case is the correct diagnosis?
- How is a new case added to the case-base?
- What should the user interface for the system look like?

Case-Based Diagnostic Systems

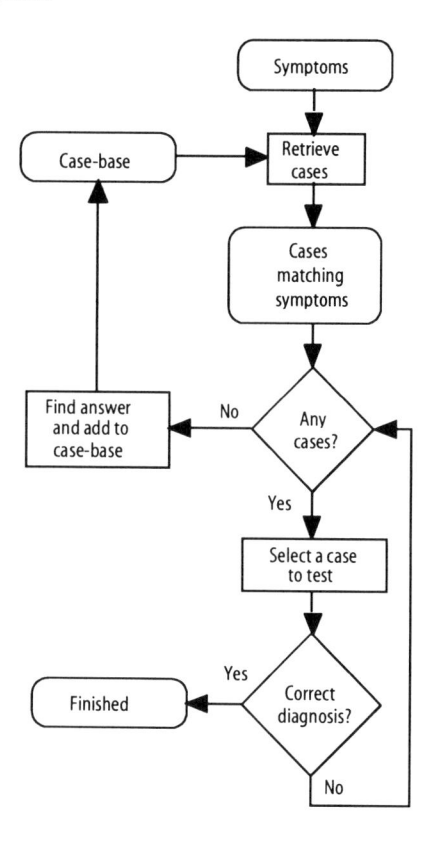

Fig. 4.1 CBR for diagnostic systems.

This chapter will give examples of effective solutions to these development questions for case-based diagnostic systems, and will illustrate how those solutions have been applied in practical systems.

4.2 CBR for Help Desk Systems

One of the reasons why CBR for help desks has been so successful is that a tool has existed for several years that made it easy to construct such systems. CBR Express, from Inference Corporation, provides a fairly limited set of CBR features. In fact, it is criticized in CBR research circles for not being a complete CBR system. However, the features that it does provide are very well suited for supplying CBR solutions to help desk problems.

CBR Express answers the CBR system-building questions raised above in the following way:

- *What kinds of past cases exist?* If all cases are logged, then there should be a case record for every significant past help desk problem. There is still an issue for the diagnostic system designer to address in deciding whether such cases are added to the case-base automatically, or in a maintenance phase.

- *How should a case be represented?* Past cases are textual records of the user's description of the symptoms, plus a textual description of the diagnosis and repair. The textual description can be annotated with tests that will confirm whether this problem is actually occurring. They can also be annotated with multimedia information about how to perform repairs. Such annotations would need to be done during a maintenance phase. On the one hand, producing these annotations greatly increases the maintenance overheads, but they can also improve the usefulness of the diagnostic system.

- *How should the symptoms be matched to past cases?* The symptoms are entered as a textual problem description. Information retrieval techniques are used to match that description against the recorded textual description of previous problems. The basic technique is to delete all words that are in a lexicon of common words ("and", "the" etc.), reduce remaining words to a stem (so that "fail" matches "failed", for example) and then measure how well the remaining words match the words in the problem description of each past case.

- *How can the matched cases be ranked for investigation?* The matching process outlined above can be employed to produce a value between 1 and 100 for each past case. The cases can then be ordered numerically, and the best matching cases investigated first.

- *How do you verify whether a case is the correct diagnosis?* If a case is annotated with a test, then the test can be used to verify whether this is the correct diagnosis. If not, then the described repair can be executed, and if the repair succeeds, then the diagnosis was correct.

- *How is a new case added to the case-base?* This depends on the designer of the diagnostic system. New cases can be added automatically, but the addition of test and repair information would have to be done separately.

- *What should the user interface for the system look like?* CBR Express provides a configurable interface. The standard version of the CBR Express interface assumes that the user has been trained to use the tool. This is not very suitable for complete beginners, but it suits the help desk situation, where the user of the system will typically be a help desk employee, talking to a remote user at the other end of a telephone line. Where end users will be running the system themselves, it is possible to customize the interface to make it easier for them to use.

The features of CBR Express can be illustrated by implementing the simple car diagnostic system in Chapter 1 as a case-based reasoning system. In order to do so, possible diagnoses must be entered as separate cases. CBR Express provides an editor to allow the entry of cases, as shown in Figure 4.2.

A case consists of a title, a description and a number of questions. The questions can either be chosen from a list of the questions that already exist, or added specifically for this case. The correct answer to each chosen question for this case must be added. It is also possible to add details of repair actions to be taken should the diagnosis prove correct.

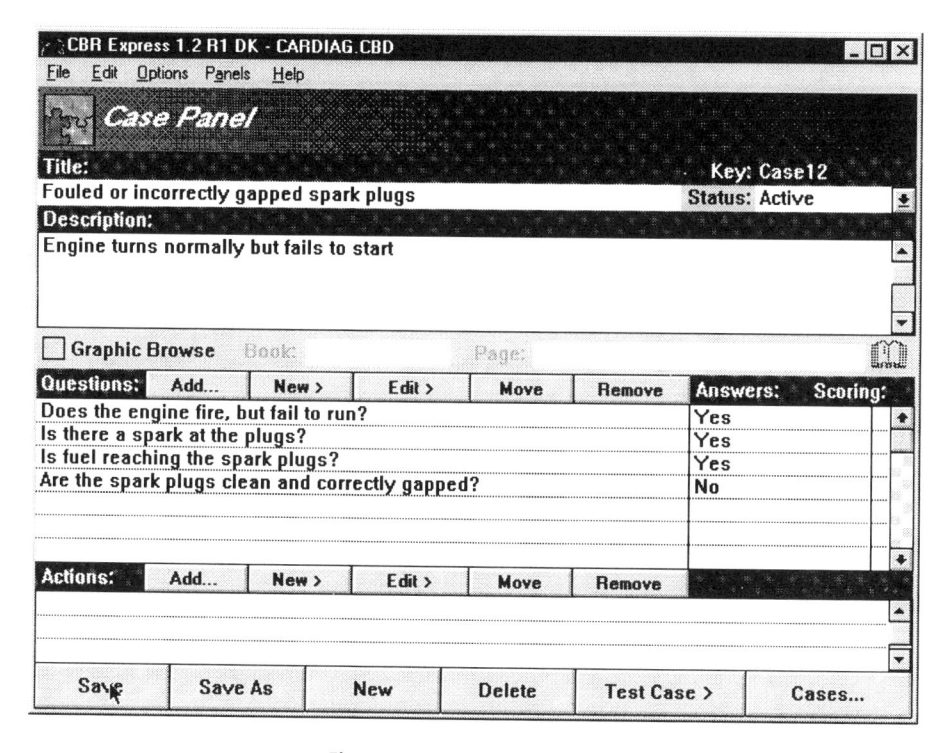

Fig. 4.2 Case editor of CBR Express.

Once the case-base exists, it can be used by typing in a description of the new problem. The description of the new problem is then matched against the description field of each existing case, and the cases that match best are shown in order, as in Figure 4.3.

It can be seen from Figure 4.3 that a reasonable match is possible even if the spelling of some of the words is incorrect. When the description was typed in, many of the cases matched very slightly. As questions are answered, some cases match more closely (because the questions have been answered in the same way as for the original case), and others with different answers are ruled out.

CBR Express does not work particularly well for this application, because the description of the cases tend to be very similar. Because of this, quite a few questions are needed to distinguish between cases, and the system builder needs to think quite hard about whether the cases can be distinguished.

In domains where there is a much wider set of symptoms (broad and shallow, as it was described earlier), case-based reasoning tends to work much better. The practical application of CBR Express to suitable diagnostic systems can be illustrated by two documented applications built by Compaq Ltd.

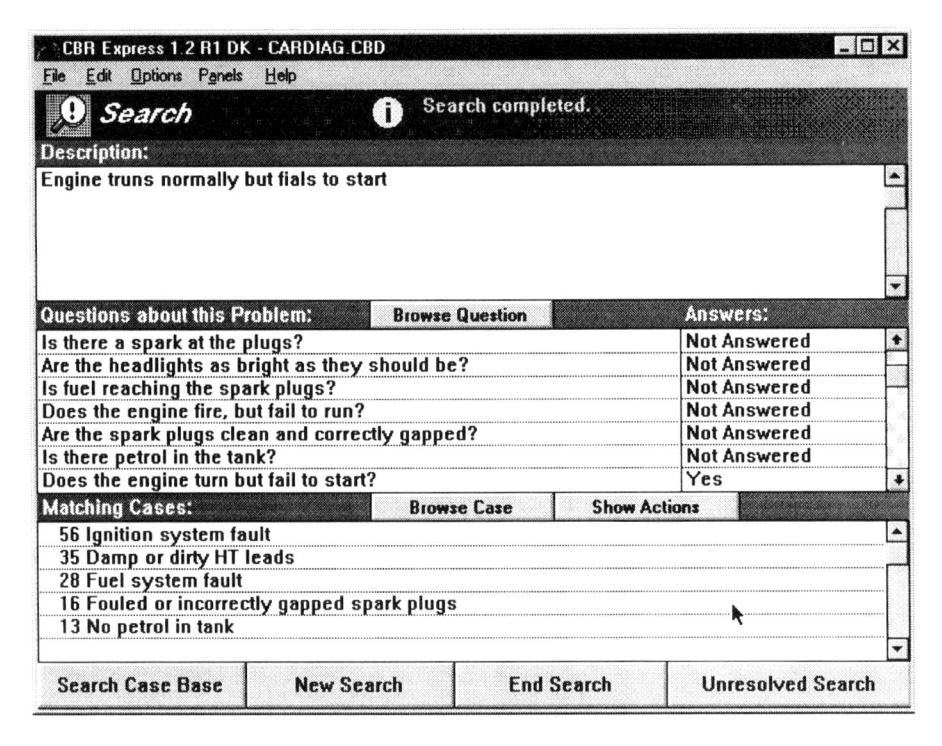

Fig. 4.3 Running the car diagnosis application.

4.2.1 Example CBR Help Desk Application 1: SMART

The SMART application (Acorn *et al.*, 1992) is an excellent example of CBR for help desk technical support based on CBR Express. SMART stands for Support Management Automated Reasoning Technology.

SMART helps Compaq customer service telephone support staff when providing technical support. The size of Compaq and the range of systems that they manufacture, from laptops to high-end systems, means that support staff need to deal with telephone requests ranging from product information requests (e.g. "Can I buy a modem for my Compaq laptop?") to problem resolution in a complex computer network ("My network has lost all machines at our Arkansas site!"). Such queries can apply to a vast array of product offerings or combinations of products.

Compaq had put a call-logging system in place as a foundation for its telephone support service. However, the increasing number and complexity of calls meant that more intelligent support for the telephone staff was needed. The SMART application fulfils that need.

SMART is linked to the call-logging database. The user's query is recorded in the call-logging database by the telephone support person (e.g. "Experiencing spurious problems in a Compaq file server, resulting in a lockup situation, ethernet topology, high traffic contention.").

If the telephone support person can provide a response for the query without using SMART, then they do so. Where the telephone support person cannot provide a satisfactory answer to the query, they can press the SMART button within the call-logging system. This invokes CBR Express with the SMART case-base.

The new query recorded in the call-logging system is used to match queries in the case-base, and likely matches are produced and ranked. The titles of the cases are displayed in likelihood order (e.g. "Banyan and System Pro with multiple server panics and lockups"). Such titles can give further clues to the support person about whether that case is likely to be relevant. As in the simple CBR Express example, relevant questions such as "What network operating system are you using?" are displayed. The telephone support engineer chooses questions to ask the customer, and the customer's answers to the questions are used to support or to rule out particular cases.

Once a case that matches the customer's problem is found, the telephone support engineer relays the information to the customer.

The session information, including the questions asked and answered and the diagnosis reached, is recorded in the resolution portion of the call log.

Where no case was found to solve the customer's problem, the session information is recorded as an unresolved case in the case-base, along with the call log number and the name of the support engineer answering the call.

Designated senior engineers have been trained as case builders. Unresolved cases are reviewed daily, and assigned to the senior engineers for resolution and incorporation into the case-base. Once the new case has been incorporated in the case-base, it is available for access by all other users.

The case-base is partitioned into a number of product lines, and several of the questions that appear (such as "What network operating system are you using?") are intended to restrict the search for matching cases to cases that apply to the same product line.

Although the amount of work being done to maintain the case-base is probably similar to that needed to maintain a rule-based diagnostic expert system, the resultant case-based system is likely to be more appropriate for this application. The problem space is not tree-shaped. It has many entry points, and textual matching of a problem description in order to decide likely problems is a better strategy than asking questions in order to try to decide where you are in a tree.

The advantages of SMART are similar to those of many successful knowledge-based system applications:

- SMART ensures that expertise is continuously available to customers and is retained within Compaq as changes of staff occur within the company.

- Customers get consistent and correct responses to their queries.
- SMART has enhanced the engineers' ability to provide timely, accurate information to customers (it takes 3–5 seconds to search for matching problems).

4.2.2 Example CBR Help Desk Application 2: QuickSource

QuickSource (Nguyen *et al.*) is another Compaq system, developing the SMART concept further. It is more specific, supporting problems with a single type of networked printer. The significant feature of QuickSource is that the case-based problem solving system is delivered with the product, so that the users can apply it themselves. Because QuickSource would be operated by end users, Compaq put a lot more thought into the user interface. They used rules to tailor CBR Express so that it did not ask so many unnecessary questions and made sure that the questions that were asked were at an appropriate level for the intended users.

The feedback from customers on provision of such support was enthusiastic. Compaq report that a conservative estimate of the effect of deploying QuickSource was savings of 20 percent of support calls for the product. A further 80 percent of the received calls to the help desk about the new product have been resolved using QuickSource.

The significant feature of QuickSource is the idea of "knowledge publishing". Instead of keeping your diagnostic knowledge in-house and having to provide help desk advice to your users, you publish the diagnostic knowledge, enabling them to meet their own needs.

Since the production of QuickSource, this idea has been changed somewhat by the emergence of the World Wide Web as a place for businesses to supply information to their customers. This is reflected in the latest version of CBR Express, which includes a run-time system for providing access to case-bases across the Web.

The market positioning of CBR Express seems to change fairly frequently, but at the time of writing, the latest version of CBR Express is called CBR3, and has been split into a number of tools, of which CBR Express is only one. They are:

- *CasePoint*. A run-time system for users of CBR3 case-bases.
- *CasePoint WebServer*. A Web-based version of CasePoint.
- *CBR Express*. The environment for developing case-bases.
- *Generator/Tester*. Tools to assist in the creation of effective case-based systems.

4.3 CBR for Complex Diagnostic Systems

Help desk systems are among the most successful diagnostic applications of case-based reasoning. That success has been based on the suitability of the technology for that kind of application, and also on the ease with which such systems can be constructed.

The technology has also been effective for other types of diagnostic application, but in application areas where more effort has been needed to build such systems.

Two successful applications are described. The first uses case-based diagnosis to support aircraft troubleshooting. The second application of case-based reasoning diagnoses problems in running an aluminum foundry.

4.3.1 Aircraft Maintenance Systems

Air Canada has a case-based reasoning system to help with the task of aircraft fleet maintenance. A fuller account of this work (Wylie *et al.*, 1997) has been given by staff at the National Research Council of Canada (NRC), who developed the case-based reasoning system.

Other commercial and military aircraft operations, including British Airways (Magaldi, 1994) have used, or are planning to use, case-based reasoning to support their aircraft maintenance operations. There are several reasons why computerized diagnostic assistance, and CBR in particular, are attractive in this domain:

- *Cost of aircraft maintenance.* Billions of dollars are spent maintaining the world's commercial airline fleets. NRC estimate that a saving of 2 percent of this budget would exceed one billion dollars a year.

- *Complexity of aircraft systems.* Modern aircraft are among the most complex of man-made systems, with different types of subsystems, many of them interacting with each other. Some method is needed of bringing together all the different types of diagnostic expertise.

- *Amount of information available.* A great deal of information exists which can be used in diagnosis (textual records of previous problems, built-in test equipment, safety requirements, written and recorded log information, troubleshooting manuals). Mastering all available information is becoming harder as newer generation monitoring equipment produces increasing amounts of potentially useful data. Relevant information must be identified and made available to the maintenance engineer.

- *Need for speed.* Aircraft maintenance is normally performed during the turnaround between flights. This is usually less than an hour. Delays can mean having to charter another aircraft, or canceling a flight. Either option is to be avoided if possible, meaning that speedy and correct diagnosis is vital.

- *Need for expertise worldwide.* Aircraft diagnosis might need to be performed at any airport to which that airline flies, but the experience available will not be equivalent at all airports. Flying an experienced engineer to a remote location will inevitably cause delays in aircraft turnaround. Automated diagnostic assistants can make the best experience consistently available worldwide.

- *Desire to forecast likely failures.* Modern aircraft have sophisticated on-board diagnostic routines. For example, the BITE (Built In Test Equipment) on an Airbus A320 generates an average of six reports per flight. Some of the messages will be actual failures, some will be minor problems, and some will be transient problems, perhaps warning of hard failures later on. Efficient classification of the different kinds of messages enables planning ahead, perhaps flying components or engineers ahead to the plane's destination, or indicating when and where preventative maintenance should take place.

The Integrated Diagnostic System (IDS) prototype is aimed at two categories of staff:

- *Line technicians.* These are the Certified Aviation Technicians (CATs) who carry out the aircraft repairs. Their main aim is to repair the aircraft in front of them as quickly as possible, taking into account the need for a safe, functional plane.
- *Maintenance operations control staff.* These are the staff who co-ordinate the maintenance effort of the whole airline fleet. They react to reports of problems with aircraft, and make higher level decisions about when and where maintenance should take place, alerting line technicians to necessary maintenance.

The main source of information for each of these categories of staff is the reports generated by the on-board diagnostic routines. Each message will have a type (either FLR for FAILURE or WRN for WARNING), a textual message and a number indicating where in the aircraft the problem has occurred. For example:

```
FLR    BRAKE TEMP SENSOR 4GW OR MONIT UNIT    2GW324715
```

There are about 3400 possible failure reports and 560 possible warning reports for an Airbus A320. When reports are generated, there are four phases of processing in the IDS:

- *Unique classification of reports.* Messages can become corrupted in transmission, and can also vary slightly. The inexact matching feature of CBR is used to match received reports against possible reports, and produce the most likely match. This works well for the types of corruption and variation that occur in reports received from the aircraft.
- *Clustering of reports.* A single failure can cause several messages. Related messages need to be grouped so that a complete picture can be gained. For example, a relay closing more slowly than expected might have caused a failure report followed by a recovery report. A rule-based system clusters the reports into a fault event. Two types of rule are used. Troubleshooting manual rules detect patterns of report that occur together and suggest probable causes for the reports. Minimum equipment list impact rules describe the conditions under which an aircraft is allowed to fly, and so alert the maintenance staff to the significance of particular failures.
- *Fault localization and initial diagnoses.* Both case-based reasoning and rules are used to decide what failures might have caused the identified fault event.

Case-Based Diagnostic Systems

- *Repair planning and reporting.* Once it is known what subsystem has failed, then it is possible to use CBR on a case-base of historical maintenance events to decide when and where to perform the necessary repairs.

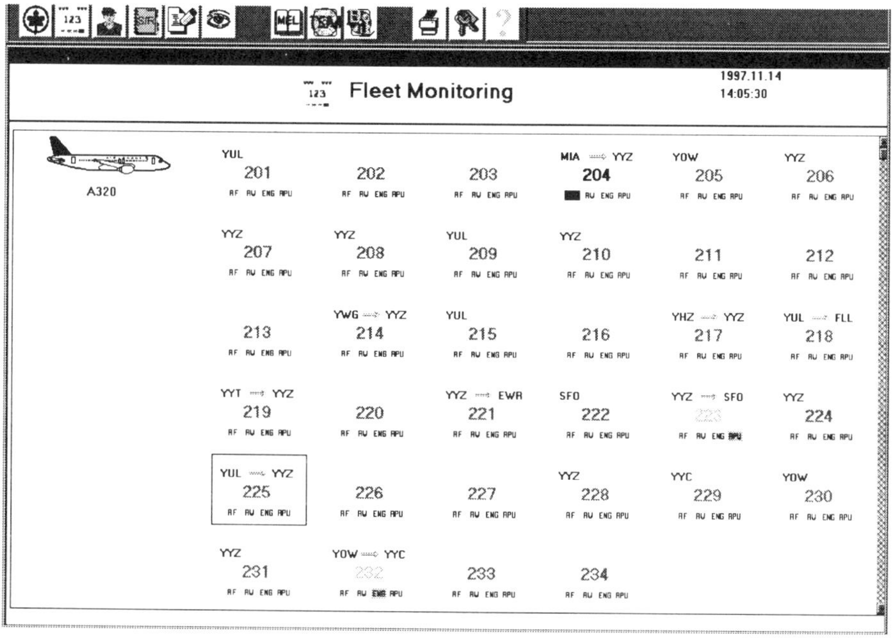

Fig. 4.4 IDS fault event monitoring screen.

The main IDS screen allows monitoring of a fleet of aircraft at once. For example, Figure 4.4 shows the following information at the top of the fourth column for the A320 aircraft with identification number 204:

Item	Meaning
MIA → YYZ	This shows where each aircraft is. This aircraft is en route from Miami (MIA) to Toronto (YYZ).
204	Unique identification number of the aircraft. Colors (and audible sounds) are used to alert operators to problems that might affect aircraft serviceability. Red represents a "NO GO" situation: the aircraft will be grounded at next station, pending some maintenance action. Yellow represents a "GO IF" situation: some diagnostic test must be performed (and passed) before the aircraft will be allowed to take off again. Grey means that the aircraft is believed to be serviceable.
AF/AV/ENG/APU	The four boxes provide information about specific subsystems (AF: airframe; AV: avionics; ENG: engines; APU: auxiliary power unit). The boxes can be colored to show the status of that area. For aircraft 204, the AF box is colored red, indicating that there is an air frame problem on this aircraft.

When the fault event monitoring screen alerts the maintenance operations control staff to the fact that there is a problem with aircraft 204, they can request further information about it. This will bring up a fault resolution screen like the one shown in Figure 4.5.

The example in Figure 4.5 shows failure reports for aircraft 207, with all rudder problem reports clustered together. The bottom half of the screen shows the different faults that might have caused the reports, along with a measure of the likelihood of each possible fault, and the action needed to repair that fault. The user can look up further information in the troubleshooting manual and other relevant databases.

Integrated diagnostic systems such as Air Canada's IDS are becoming vital as the complexity of modern aircraft increases. Case-based reasoning provides an excellent way of recording diagnostic experience of many different kinds of failures and making it available for use in future problem solving.

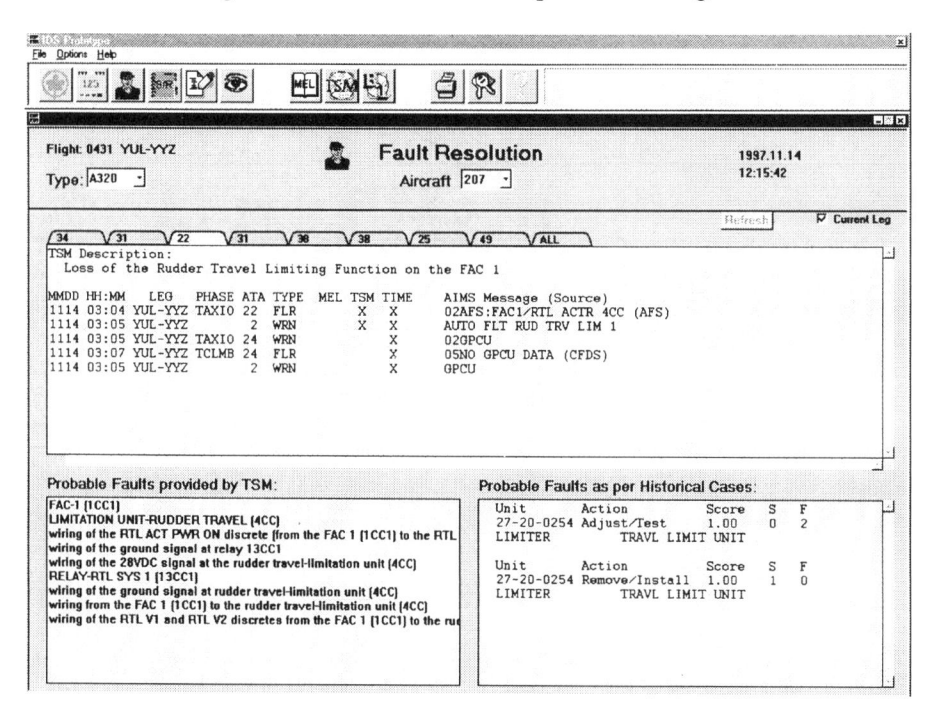

Fig. 4.5 IDS fault resolution screen.

4.3.2 Foundry Troubleshooting System

The section describes the use of case-based reasoning to troubleshoot process problems in aluminum foundries. While this example is in a foundry, the general principle of using quality control procedures to monitor the construction of a case-base and to feed that knowledge back into process design applies to many industries. It is especially relevant to first- and second-tier suppliers of other companies, as quality feedback comes directly to the supplier, rather than being received second- or third-hand via a distributor or dealer.

The Pressure Die Casting Process

The machines used to cast aluminum vary in the way they operate. Most machines inject the metal from the side, others from the top. In addition, a vacuum system can be used to drain air from the cavity prior to casting, in order to lessen the effect of air pockets in the casting. Larger machines would be used to cast heavier or more complex parts. The characteristics of the die can also vary, from a simple die of two halves, to a more intricate system with sliders and cores that allow more complex shapes to be cast. Some dies contain multiple impressions of the same part, so that several can be made during one casting cycle.

The components produced by aluminum die-casters are typically finished products. The process of casting the metal is only one of a long list of operations including processes such as:

- clipping;
- milling;
- drilling;
- powder coating;
- inspection;
- storage;
- transportation.

Each of these processes is subject to different kinds of failures. Although the kinds of process problems that occur are similar from one foundry to another, the methods used to tackle the problems can be foundry-specific. Because there are different approaches to casting, building a general rule-based troubleshooting system for foundries would be difficult. Troubleshooting requires detailed knowledge of design constraints, customer requirements and the manufacturing process as implemented at the particular foundry. This means that troubleshooting information is often foundry specific, and best expressed as records of past cases.

Recording Foundry Problems

The foundry process troubleshooting system was based on an existing paper-based process concern report (PCR) quality control system, where process problems were recorded on paper and tracked until they were solved. In the worst cases, a truckload of aluminum components might be returned from a customer because of some problem such as bad surface finish.

The foundry staff would need to:

- record the return of stock;
- check the quality of further components of the same type made since the delivery;
- identify whether the problem was still occurring and fix it;
- decide what could be done with the returned stock;
- plan what to do to avoid repetition of the problem in future.

The computerized version of the PCR system can record problems in a database, and has links to other foundry databases in order to make entry of information as painless as possible; for example, by entering a component name, the PCR system pulls in customer details. The problem is described by selecting the process name from a list of processes, and then selecting a problem type from a list of possible problems with that process. In addition, free text may also be used to describe the problem. An example of a problem specification is given in Figure 4.6.

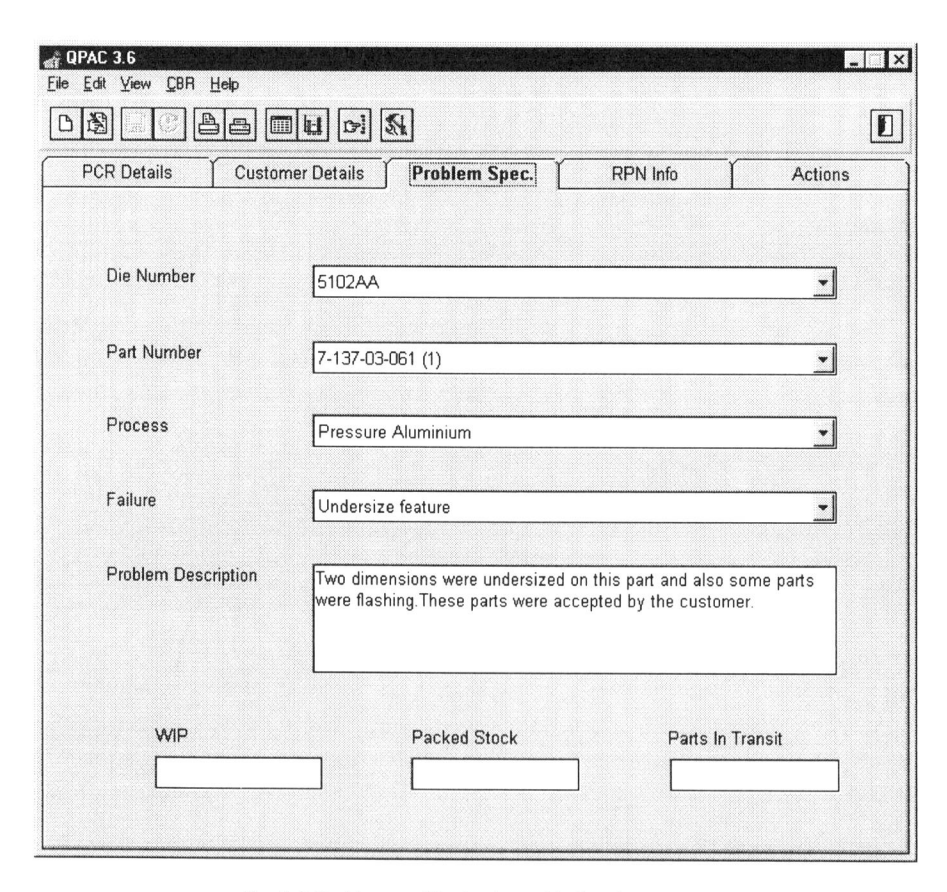

Fig. 4.6 Problem specification in troubleshooting system.

Matching Past Problems

When the basic problem description has been entered, the user can choose to perform case-based matching against previous similar problems. Cases in the PCR system are flat database records. Case matching is done by nearest neighbor, and produces a list of possibly relevant cases by a weighted match on:

- type of the process in which the problem occurred;
- specific problem with the process;
- component category;
- component attributes;
- recentness of past problem.

A list of matches like the one shown in Figure 4.7 is produced. The user can look through this list and examine the detailed record of each past case, using their judgement to select the most appropriate of the matches. The component category matching is based on a component hierarchy, and is used to order the cases in such a way that the most likely cases will be those as close as possible in the hierarchy to the problem.

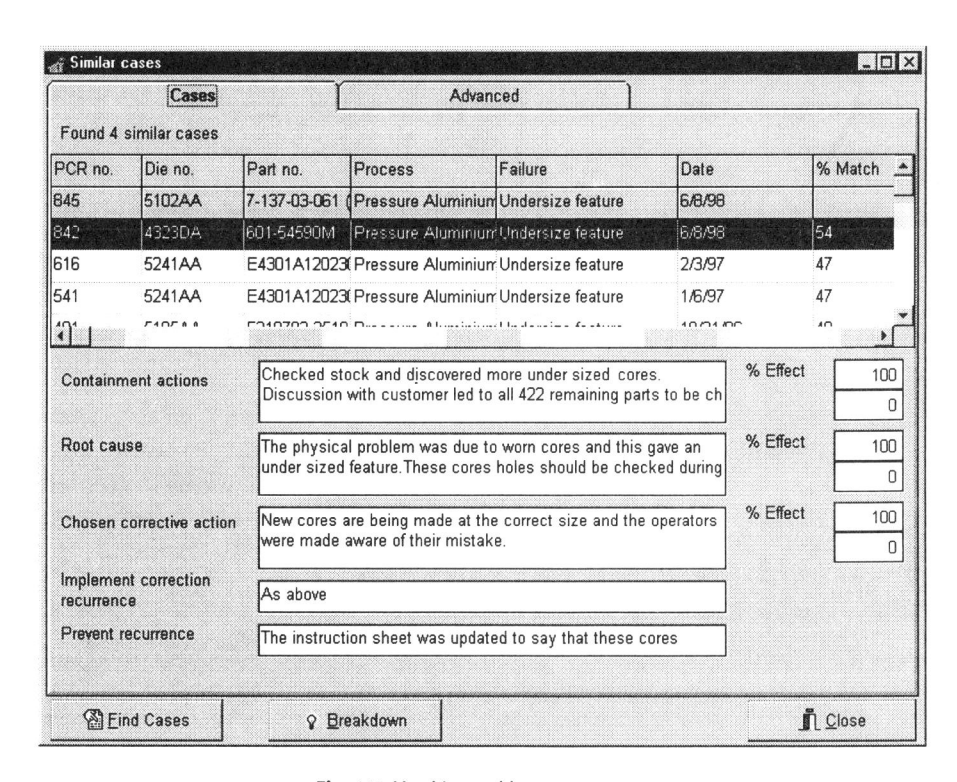

Fig. 4.7 Matching problem to past cases.

Classifying the components manufactured at the foundries involved investigation of the quality demands required of different types of component. Different categories with identical quality demands were merged. The process of building the classification tree was an iterative one requiring a great deal of consultation with quality managers.

When a good match with a past case is found, details of the actions taken last time can be imported to the present case, providing information on matters such as the appropriate team of people to deal with the problem, the actions needed to solve the problem and the most efficient way to handle faulty components that have already been manufactured.

As well as providing painless entry of information, the foundry staff have been encouraged to use the PCR system by provision of facilities such as automated faxing of problem report acknowledgements to customers, and problem tracking facilities for quality managers to monitor the progress of solutions to problems.

The PCR system has been installed at three aluminum foundries that run similar computing facilities. Each foundry presently has a three-figure number of cases recorded, and uses the system to record, track and help fix all problems that occur.

One of the notable features of the PCR system is that no outside support for case-based maintenance is needed. All problems are eventually fixed, and when they are, the foundry quality manager "closes" the problem report. The act of closing a problem report essentially validates the case associated with that problem report, saying that an acceptable solution has been found. Only closed (and therefore validated) reports are matched in case-based matching. The foundry quality managers are validating the case-base while carrying out their normal function.

Structure of Case

The structure of the entities used in the case-base has been defined using the EXPRESS information modeling language (Schenck et al., 1994). The following is a simplification of the EXPRESS description for a case.

```
(* definition of abstract PCR *)
ENTITY QPAC_PCR
    date_raised: date;
    customer: business;
    customer_contact: person;
    foundry_contact: foundry_person;
    die_number: die_num_type;
    part_number: part_num_type;
    process_area: process_type;
    problem: problem_type;
    severity: severity_type;
    reaction: reaction_type;
    occurrence: percentage;-- percentage of parts affected
    quantity: whole_number;-- number of parts affected
    description: strings;
    actions: LIST [1:?] OF action;
```

```
WHERE
    problem_ok:
        applicable(problem,process_area);
END_ENTITY; -- end of top level PCR entity

(* entity to define a simple action *)
ENTITY action;
    action_by: foundry_person;
    action_taken: action_taken_type;
    action_status: action_status_type;
END_ENTITY;

action_status: (for_information_only,
                further_action_required,
                success,
                failure);
```

The cases are stored using a DBASE3 database. Case matching and retrieval is done by database access and weighted matching.

The CBR system described here is part of a larger system that closes the loop from diagnostic troubleshooting back to design. The cases are not just used to perform diagnosis of existing problems, but to help avoid the same problems occurring in new designs. Figure 4.8 illustrates the central role that the PCR case-base plays in troubleshooting and in design.

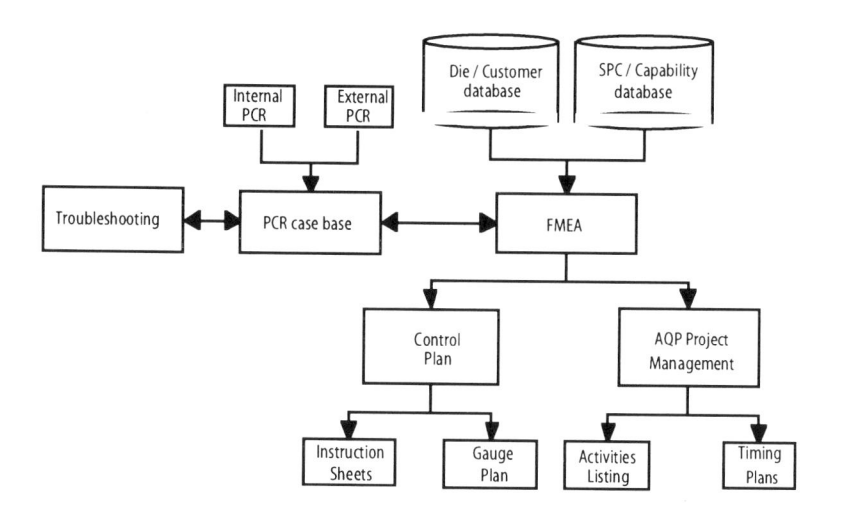

Fig. 4.8 Overall troubleshooting/design perspective.

The Process Concern Report case-base stores problem information from inside and outside the foundry, along with the solutions to those problems. This information can be used immediately for problem solving, but also feeds into the process failure modes and effects analysis (FMEA) of new dies. When a new die is being designed, all of the failures that could happen on such a die should be considered. The PCR database provides realistic information about what are the significant failures that actually have happened on similar dies in this foundry. This information tells the designers what problems they need to design out of the new process. Where this cannot be done, then they can plan for fault detection by inspection and measurement.

Thus it can be seen that case-based reasoning provides the foundation for allowing troubleshooting knowledge to be built up and re-used for quality-related procedures. It provides excellent data for creating a realistic process FMEA report, and even beyond that, for deciding on inspection and control checks in the foundry itself.

The largest of the foundries where the case-based system described in this chapter has been implemented has less than 400 employees. Even in companies of this size, CBR provides a valuable repository of past decisions, and feeding that experience into future designs is proving valuable. The potential for this kind of system should be even greater in large companies where knowledge is more widely diffused through the organization.

4.4 Summary of Case-Based Reasoning

Case-based reasoning is an excellent way of building diagnostic systems where there is a wide range of possible problems. A textual description of the problem can be used to narrow down the search to a smaller number of past problems, and then questions related to the likely past problems can be asked in order to identify the exact problem. The recorded solution to the identified past problem can then be used as a solution for the new problem. This type of diagnostic system has proved very effective in the help desk situation, as a support tool for customer support staff. A recent extension of that concept has been to deliver the diagnostic tool to the customer, relieving the burden on support staff. Early experience is that computer literate customers are likely to use such a tool, where they would have been more reluctant to read the same information presented in the form of a manual.

Several situations do not favor the use of case-based reasoning. Where the diagnostic system must diagnose a large complex device, then case-based reasoning has several problems that may not make it suitable for such a system. If the device has just been designed, then there may not be information on relevant past diagnoses, and so no material with which to build a case-base. Efficient diagnosis might also demand the investigation of possible failures in a particular order (as illustrated by the elevator diagnosis problem in Chapter 3). Where that is the case, although most case-based reasoning tools will allow the user to specify the order in which questions are asked, it is less effort to use a tool such as Grade to explicitly arrange the investigation of possible faults.

5. *Model-Based Diagnostic Systems*

In this chapter, we shall consider the use of models as a basis for diagnosis. The general idea is that the model predicts what should be happening in the observed device, and that discrepancies between the model of the device and the observed device can be used to detect problems and to decide what might be causing the problems.

In order to build a model-based diagnostic system, there are several basic design decisions to be made:

- What kinds of model should be used?
- What aspects of the domain should be modeled?
- What kind of diagnostic framework should be built?

This chapter will consider each of these issues in turn, constructing a picture of how models and diagnostic strategy can come together to produce a model-based diagnostic system. The following chapter will give detailed examples of how these items have been linked in some practical model-based systems.

5.1 Choosing What to Model for Model-Based Diagnosis

The example of a simple car headlight circuit shown in Figure 5.1 contains two sets of lights: the main headlights and the fog lamps. When the main headlight switch is closed, the main headlights come on. When both switches are open, or just the fog lamp switch is closed, no lights are on. When the main headlight switch is closed and the fog lamp switch is closed, both sets of lamps are on.

There are a number of different types of models of this circuit that could be used. The diagnostic tasks that can be accomplished by model-based reasoning will depend on the type of model chosen.

We will consider four kinds of model:

- simple dependency models;
- state-based models;

- component-based circuit models, no faults simulated;
- component-based circuit models with fault models.

Each type of model has its own advantages and drawbacks, and often the choice of model will depend on the characteristics of the domain being modeled and on the information easily available in the domain. The simple car lighting circuit in Figure 5.1 will be used as an example for each kind of model, but the advantages and drawbacks of each kind of modeling will be considered for other types of diagnostic application as well. The models grow in complexity through the examples, and it will be seen that some of the more complex models, where available, can be used to produce the simpler ones.

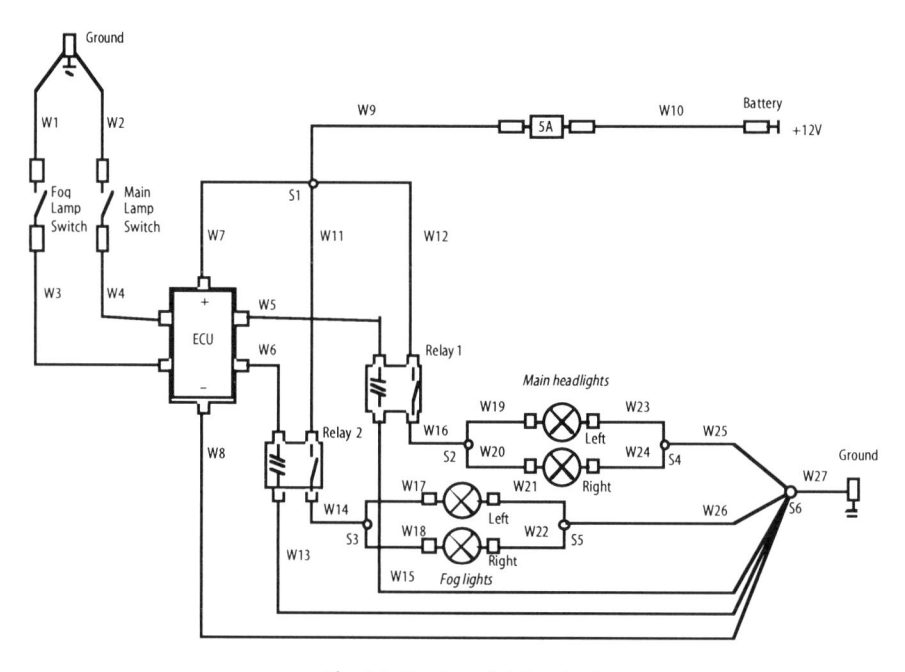

Fig. 5.1 Simple car lighting circuit.

Each type of model will tend to focus on the components in the circuit in some way, because the final goal of diagnosis on the circuit will be to localize diagnosis to a single component, or at any rate to a *least replaceable unit* (LRU). A LRU is the smallest unit to which diagnosis needs to be done, because it is the level at which repair is carried out. For example, a fault may be due to a failed resistor, but if the repair action is to replace the circuit board containing the resistor, then diagnosis need only go as far as the board level. Where several components are packed together into a module, then an LRU might contain several components, and practical diagnosis would want to take that into account. For all of the types of model, the idea of a *suspect* or a *candidate fault* is used: a failure of the circuit that could account for the observed behavior.

In other domains, such as gas turbines or chemical plants, where what is being modeled and diagnosed is a process rather than a device, models may not focus on physical components in the same way. In such domains, the modeling primitives might be subprocesses, but the same types of principles can be applied.

In Figures 5.1 and 5.2, items with names beginning with "W" are wires, and items with names beginning with "S" are splices, which join several wires together. ECU denotes an Electronic Control Unit, essentially a computer in the car, used to control the operation of the car. An ECU will typically be much more complex than pictured here, with perhaps 64 or 128 pins, but only the pins relevant to the use of the ECU in this circuit have been portrayed. The function of the ECU in the circuit pictured in Figure 5.1 is to link the operation of the two switches, only enabling the fog lamps when both switches are closed.

5.1.1 Simple Dependency Model

In this type of model, all that is expressed is the fact that the correct working of one component depends on a number of others. In essence, what is formed is a tree of dependencies, with the most important components (often the components where the symptoms are observable) at the top of the tree.

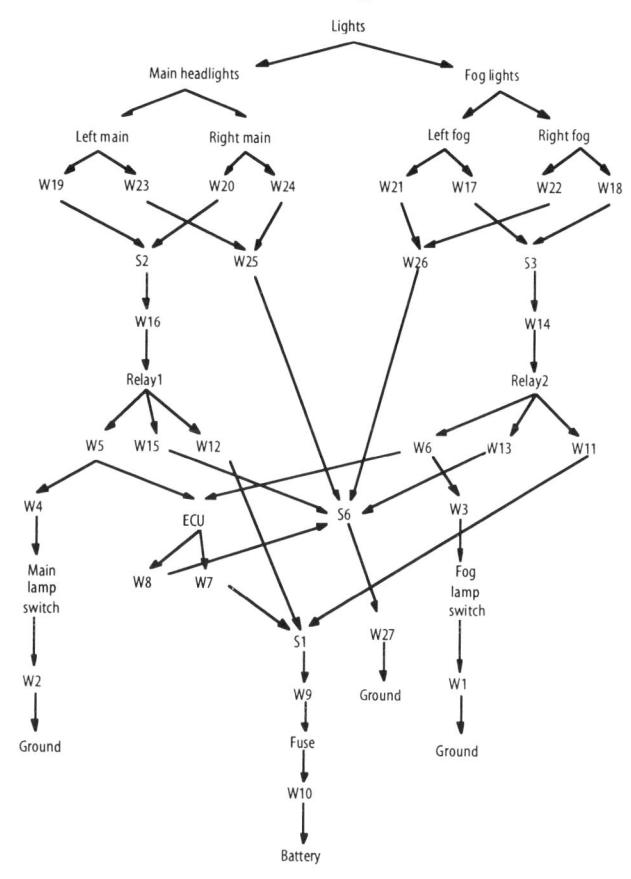

Fig. 5.2 Dependency graph for simple car lighting circuit.

Figure 5.2 shows the dependencies for the simple car lighting circuit. As this example illustrates, the relationships actually form a graph rather than a tree: branches can join together again. This particular example is an acyclic graph: there are no mutual dependencies between components. In general, there can be mutual dependencies. For example, if there is a feedback loop in a system, such dependencies will exist, and it can be difficult to diagnose such situations because every component in the loop depends on every other component.

In the example graph in Figure 5.2, the top levels of the tree are slightly different from the lower levels. They are not components, and so cannot be the cause of the problem. They are in the dependency graph in order to focus the search for possible suspects. Using the terms outlined in Chapter 2, the top levels of the tree are in the graph in order to perform problem identification and fault localization, whereas the lower levels assist with fault identification.

At the lower levels, some choices have been made on how to represent the dependencies. Following the topology of the circuit, it would have been possible to put W3 and W4 (the input signals to the ECU) under the ECU. However, the correct behavior of the ECU does not depend on these things: if W3 fails, then the ECU can still turn on the main beams correctly. For this reason, W5 is portrayed as dependent on W4, rather than the ECU being dependent on W4.

A depth first algorithm for using this type of graph for diagnosis would be:

```
Add the root of the tree to list of suspects.
REPEAT
    Take suspect at front of list.
    Test if the suspect is working correctly.
        If it is, then delete it from the list of candidates.
        If it is not, then
            Test if suspect component itself is faulty.
            If it is, then fault is identified.
            If not,
                Delete suspect from the list of candidate faults
                Add all items that depend on the suspect to the front of the list of suspects
UNTIL list of suspects is empty or fault is identified.
```

This might work in the following way for the case where the right fog lamp was not working because wire W22 was not connected to the fog lamp:

```
Add "Lights" to the list of suspects.
"Lights" is not directly testable, so delete it and add its dependants.
Test if "Main headlights" working. They are OK, so delete from list.
Test if "Fog lights" working. They are not.
"Fog lights" are not testable for faults, so delete and add dependants.
Test if "Left fog" is working. It is, so delete it.
Test if "Right fog" is working. It is not.
Test whether "Right fog" lamp is faulty by connecting a power supply directly to it. It lights up, so the
    lamp is OK.
Delete "Right fog lamp" and add its dependants (W22, W18).
Test whether W22 is working (does it supply current to the fog lamp when expected). It is not working.
Test whether W22 is faulty (does the wire conduct current and is it connected at both ends?).
W22 is not connected at the fog lamp. Fault is identified.
```

Practical considerations bring several complications to this simple scheme. Some of the complications are concerned with testing. One problem is that the strategy may not lead to efficient location of the failure. Some tests may be much more expensive to perform than others, and one would wish to use that information to order tests more sensibly. In order to do that, a more flexible strategy, which keeps track of all possible suspects and orders them efficiently, is needed. This can be achieved by using the concepts of *suspect generation* and *suspect exoneration*.

The first algorithm described above had a simple method for suspect generation, generating as few suspects as possible. Another way of controlling diagnosis for this kind of model is to generate all possible suspects, and then to rank the investigation of suspects according to likelihood.

Exoneration is a useful concept here: if a component known to be working correctly depends on another component, then the other component can be assumed to be working correctly. This allows the dismissal of large numbers of suspects. In this scheme, the top levels of the tree, used for problem identification and fault localization have to be treated differently from the components. They are termed symptoms in the following algorithm:

> Add root of tree to list of suspect symptoms.
>
> WHILE list of suspect symptoms is not empty
> Test symptom.
> If it is not OK:
>   If its dependants are symptoms:
>   then add its dependants to the list of suspect symptoms
>   If its dependants are components
>   then add its dependants to the list of suspect components
> If it is OK:
>   then add it to the list of OK symptoms
> Delete the symptom from the list of suspect symptoms
>
> For each suspect component, recursively add all components dependent on that component to the list of suspect components unless they are already on the list of suspect components.
>
> For each OK symptom, recursively follow the dependency tree under the symptom, and remove any components encountered from the list of suspect components.
>
> Order the remaining suspect components according to likelihood of guilt, cost of test, etc., and investigate in turn. Where a component is investigated and found to work correctly, then further exoneration can be performed if the component's correct behavior depends on other components in the list of suspects.

For the example given earlier of a problem with wire W22, this would work in the following way:

> Add "Lights" to the list of suspect symptoms.
> "Lights" are not OK, so add "Main headlights" and "Fog lights" to list of suspects, and delete "Lights"
> "Main headlights" are OK: add to list of OK symptoms, and delete from suspects.
> "Fog lights" are not OK, add "Left fog lamp" and "Right fog lamp" to list of suspects, and delete "Fog lights".
> "Left fog lamp" is OK. Add to list of OK symptoms and delete from list of suspects.
> "Right fog lamp" is not OK, add to list of suspects.

At this point, the list of suspects is "Right fog lamp", and the list of OK symptoms is "Main headlights" and "Left fog lamp". Suspect generation and exoneration can then be performed on this initial position.

> From "Right fog lamp", a full list of 25 suspects can be generated: (Right fog lamp, W22, W26, S6, W27, Ground connection from W27, W18, S3, W14, Relay 2, W6, ECU, W8, W7, W3, Fog lamp switch, W1, Ground connection from W1, W13, W11, S1, W9, Fuse, W10, Battery).
>
> From the OK symptom list, Main headlights exonerates 11 of those suspects: (S6, W27, Ground connection from W27, ECU, W8, W7, S1, W9, Fuse, W10, Battery). Left fog light exonerates a further 11 suspects: (W26, S3, W14, Relay 2, W6, W3, Fog lamp switch, W1, Ground connection from W1, W13, W11).
>
> This leaves just three suspects: (Right fog lamp, W22, W18).
>
> The three suspects can then be ranked and investigated.

One of the dangers of this approach is that exonerated candidates may actually be to blame. For example, a splice could crack in such a way that some connections were still OK, but others were not. A more robust method would be not to rule out suspects that were exonerated, but to rank them lower than any other suspects. Using the more robust method on the example of a failure because W22 is not connected, the same result would be achieved as efficiently, but if the problem had been a bad splice, rather than a disconnected wire, then it would have still been discovered.

Advantages of Simple Dependency Models

- *They are easy to build.* The only kind of information in the model is that the correct working of one component depends on the correct working of a number of others.

- *They do not need explicit reasoning about the domain.* It is possible to build dependency models mixing electrical systems with processes and mechanical systems. This is much more challenging to achieve for some of the more complex types of modeling.

- *They can often be automatically generated.* For the example system used in this chapter, the dependency diagram might be automatically generated from the topology of the circuit, as long as the implicit connections through the ECU are declared.

- *Diagnosis with these models is easy to implement.* The simple algorithms above can be easily coded, and refined to fit particular circumstances.

Disadvantages of Simple Dependency Models

- *They are hard to verify.* If the models are built by hand, then it is difficult to see whether the dependencies are correct. That is true even for the simple circuit in Figure 5.1, which is a drastic simplification of real automobile lighting circuits. Even there, several errors were spotted after producing a supposedly correct dependency chart: splice S5 has been missed out, and the correct operation of wire W5 depends on W3 as well as W4. Building dependency models by hand is not a sensible option for large complex systems.

- *They do not have enough information to decide what tests to perform.* For example, to check whether the right fog lamp is working will involve turning both sets of lights on, with the ignition on as well. This model does not contain that information, and so test information needs to be expressed some other way.

- *There is not enough information to make some deductions.* For example, dependency models do not use information about whether the problem is a function not happening or an unexpected function happening. This can be used to rule out some components. For example, if a lamp comes on when it is not expected, then one would examine wires for shorts to battery, but would not examine the lamp for a hidden power supply.

- *Failures can change the dependency diagram.* A classic example of this for car circuitry is when a ground stud detaches from the car body. The effect can be to change much of the functionality of the system, and the dependency diagram becomes incorrect. Such circumstances are fairly rare, but do occur.

5.1.2 State-Based Model

It is possible to characterize many systems in terms of the possible states that the system can be in. The states are linked by the transitions that cause the system to move from state to state, forming a state graph or state transition chart.

In the example of the simple car headlight circuit, the correct behavior of the circuit can be described by the state graph in Figure 5.3. The transitions are the possible changes to the two switches controlling the circuit. The states show which switches are closed in that state, and which lamps are lit.

The state graph summarizes and clarifies the informal description of the circuit's activity given earlier. The state change where the fog lamp switch is closed, but the fog lamps give no light because the main beams are not switched on, can be clearly seen. In this example, the behavior of the system only depends on the combination of switches that are closed. If it also depended on the order in which they were closed (for example, if the fog lamps only became active if the main headlight switch was closed *before* the fog lamp switch was closed), then that would also be evident from this state graph.

A clear description of the correct operation of the system can be vital for effective model-based diagnosis, because it enables problem identification and some degree of fault localization. For example, the incorrect behavior of the circuit when wire W22 is not connected can be described by the state graph in Figure 5.4. The disconnected wire means that the right fog lamp will fail to light, and so where one would expect both fog lamps to be on, only the left fog lamp will be lit.

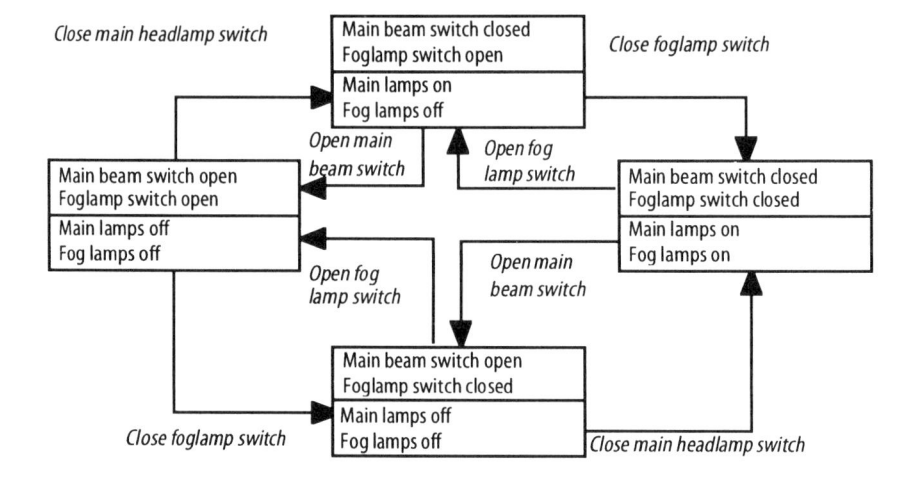

Fig. 5.3 State graph for simple car lighting circuit.

Such a description could be obtained by guiding the user through the correct working of the system and obtaining discrepancies. For example, "close the main beam switch: do the main lamps light?"

Once the state graph for the faulty circuit has been obtained, it can be compared with the correct state graph to localize possible failures. In this example, because the main lamps work when they are expected, diagnosis can concentrate on suspects that do not affect the main lamps, but do affect the fog lamps (and especially the right fog lamp).

The state graph has provided us with a method for identifying which functions are affected by the failure, but does not provide any information on which suspects might have caused the failure – other models such as dependency models are needed for that.

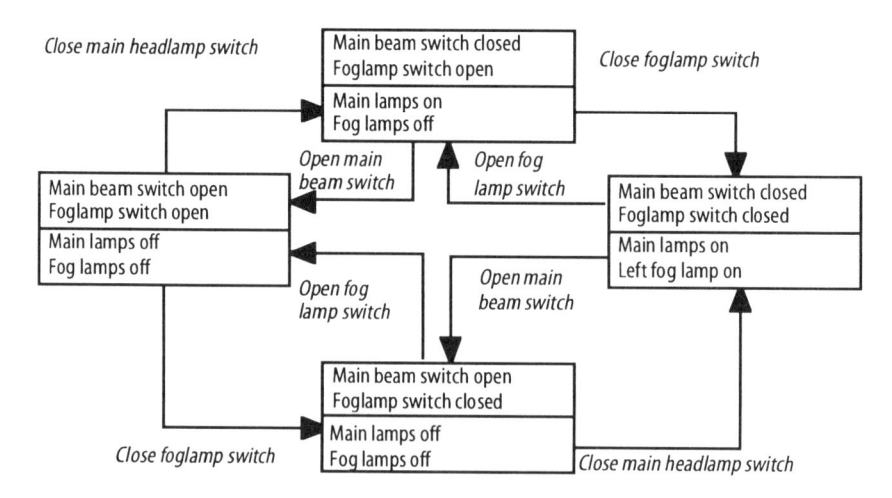

Fig. 5.4 State graph for faulty car lighting circuit.

Advantages of State-Based Models

- *They are easy to build.* They express the overall behavior of the whole system. Such descriptions will often exist at design time, if only in a textual form. The state graph will often be less ambiguous than a textual description, and so there are some other advantages to producing state graphs during the design process. Several design tools, such as StateMate from Ilogix, can be used to produce such design descriptions.

- *They imply which tests to perform for problem identification.* The state graph describes the correct operation of the system, and can be used to guide the user through the correct operation and to identify where behavioral discrepancies occur.

- *They provide a focus for fault localization.* Once behavioral discrepancies have been identified, then they can be used to identify functions of the system that are working correctly, and functions which are not. This information gives a basis for the type of suspect generation and exoneration outlined earlier using dependency models.

Disadvantages of State-Based Models

- *They are not linked to the components of the system.* They only describe links between the inputs and outputs of the system. They tell us nothing about the expected state of many of the components within the system.

- *They are insufficient for performing fault identification and fault diagnosis.* While they provide a focus for fault localization, knowledge of the internal workings of the system is also needed to perform fault identification – if only at the level provided by a dependency graph. Knowledge about the state of individual components is needed to decide what tests to perform during fault diagnosis. Such knowledge needs other kinds of models.

5.1.3 Component-Based Circuit Model, No Faults

Both of the types of model discussed so far have needed to be built manually for the overall circuit. Where a large circuit has complex behavior, such models can take a great deal of construction. One of the main goals of model-based diagnosis is to use the structure of the domain to synthesize the overall behavior. For electrical circuits, the structure is often easily available from a circuit diagram. By providing descriptions of typical electrical components, simulation can be used to decide the overall behavior of the circuit. When such simulation can be achieved, dependency graphs and state graphs can both be generated from the results of the simulation and used in diagnosis.

There are several dimensions to choosing a suitable model (*What is a component in this domain? At what level should components be modeled?*), and these questions are considered in Section 5.2. For the rest of Section 5.1, I will only consider how component modeling can be achieved in the electrical domain, using qualitative models of components (models that reason only about whether current is flowing or not, and do not attempt to calculate values for the current). A structural description of the circuit is often available on-line for car circuits, because of the use of electrical computer-aided design (CAD) to design the circuit. Individual components can usually be identified as the items that are drawn separately in the CAD tool: wires, relays, motors, lamps etc. The circuit in Figure 5.1 contains nine different types of component:

- wire;
- switch;
- relay;
- lamp;
- splice;
- fuse;
- battery;
- ground;
- electronic control unit (ECU).

The behavior of each of these types of component can be described generically except for the ECU. All other components can be described in such a way that they can be used in any circuit, but ECU behavior tends to be very dependent on what it is being used for. For example, an ECU in a car might have 64 pins and that ECU might be involved in the behavior of a dozen different circuits within the car. Within a single circuit such as the example one, perhaps only half a dozen of those pins are used, and so only a small part of its behavior needs to be described. That means that it is far more sensible to describe the behavior of an ECU that is specific to a circuit, rather than to attempt to describe the overall behavior of the whole ECU.

The description of component behavior that is needed for each type of component will have three separate aspects:

- *Terminals.* Terminals are the inputs and outputs for the component. They are the points where other components can connect to this component.
- *Internal topology of component.* The functionality of the component is determined in terms of links between terminals. These links can include logical resistors whose resistance value can change depending on the state of other parts of the component.
- *Dependencies.* Dependencies define how the values of the internal resistors of a component change as the state of the other parts of the component change.

Behavior for a Switch

The switch has two terminals. The terminals can be regarded as joined by a variable resistor whose value depends on the state of the switch. When the switch is open, then the resistor has infinite resistance. When the switch is closed, the resistor has zero resistance.

Behavior for an Open Relay

An open relay is composed of a coil and a switch whose state depends on the state of the coil. When current flows through the coil, the switch is closed, otherwise it is open.

Such a relay has four terminals, two to the coil and two to the relay switch. The coil will be a fixed resistor, and the switch resistor will be variable and depend on the state of the coil. When the state of the coil is Active, that is, current is flowing through it, then the value of the switch resistor is zero because the switch is closed. When the state of the coil is Inactive, that is, no current is flowing through it, then the value of the switch resistor is infinite as the switch is open.

Behavior for a Wire

A wire has two terminals, one at each end. If one end of the wire is connected to the battery and the other end to ground, then current is flowing through the wire.

ECU Behavior in the Example Circuit

The ECU in the example circuit has six terminals, two to supply power to the ECU, and two inputs and two outputs connected by variable resistors to the battery. The values of the resistors on the outputs are defined as infinite, unless there is power to the ECU and the relevant input(s) are Active.

Given these kinds of descriptions and information about the state of switches and sensors, it is possible to calculate where current is flowing in a circuit, and in which direction. This gives a snapshot of circuit activity, but for some components, such as the ECU and the relays, the fact that parts of the circuit are active will cause changes to take place in the circuit state; for example, relays may close. Where such events occur, it is necessary to recalculate the state of the circuit until either the circuit is stable or a set of states is repeated.

In the case of the example circuit, closing the main headlight switch will cause the input to the ECU through wire W4 to become active (because it is now connected to ground). The ECU will then make the output through W5 to be connected to battery. The coil through Relay 1 and W15 is now active, so the switch of Relay 1 will close. This means that the Left and Right main headlights are now connected to the battery and ground, and will be active.

This example illustrates that the kind of behavioral component description given for electrical components can be used to reason about the behavior of the overall circuit, using the connection information provided in the structural diagram of the circuit. How can this simulation be used for diagnosis?

Essentially, the simulation can be used to produce the two types of information described in Sections 5.1.1 and 5.1.2 (dependency graphs and state graphs), and then it can be used in the same way as that information would be used.

A dependency graph for the circuit can be obtained by recording the dependencies between components when performing simulation. So for example, the left main lamp will light because there is current through: battery, W10, Fuse, W9, S1, W12, Relay 1, W16, S2, W19, S4, W25, S6, W27, and Ground. Therefore the left main lamp is dependent on those items. Relay 1 in turn is dependent on current through the ECU, W5, W15, S6, W27, and Ground components. The ECU will have a similar set of dependencies. A dependency graph of the type described in Section 5.1.1 can be constructed when performing simulation by observing the dependencies between components. The starting point for such a graph should be the externally observed items – the lamps in the case of this example – and so these must be identified in some way.

A state graph for the circuit can be obtained by trying every change of input for the circuit, and recording the state of each component after the change of input has happened. However, that would be very verbose – even the example circuit has 45 components. Some way of identifying the important components needs to be provided, and then the state of the device can be defined in terms of the state of those components. As Figure 5.3 implies, for the simple circuit example, it is only the state of the input switches and the lamps themselves that are interesting.

Both for generating dependency graphs and for generating useful state graphs, it is necessary to be able to declare which components of the circuit are 'interesting' outside of the circuit. This can be done in a device-independent way by declaring the functions of the circuit, and then defining which component states imply that the functions are happening.

For the example circuit, the interesting functions are main headlights and fog lights. Those functions would be the same, no matter how the function was implemented. For example, if the fog lights were implemented as a fluorescent strip light, then the strip light would still be fulfilling the fog lights' function. What changes for each implementation of the function is how it is fulfilled. In the example circuit, it is fulfilled when the left fog lamp is Active and the right fog lamp is Active.

Such a function definition gives an important starting point for generating dependency graphs and state graphs, in the manner discussed above.

Advantages of Component-Based Circuit Models without Faults

- *They allow simulation of the activity of the circuit.* This can be important, in order to verify that the system being described matches the working system.

Model-Based Diagnostic Systems

- *They enable the principled construction of state graphs and dependency graphs.* This means that they can perform all of the problem identification, fault localization and fault identification tasks of those graphs, as described earlier in this chapter. The construction of state graphs and dependency graphs is also performed consistently, which is unlikely to be the case when such graphs are constructed manually.

- *They provide information for deciding on tests.* Given some external observations, simulation of the correctly working circuit can be used to decide on tests to be performed on the circuit. For example, the simulation says that the only state in which to test whether the fog lamps are working is the one where both switches are closed. At a lower level, the simulation can provide information on what tests should be performed on individual components to find out whether they are working as expected.

- *Reuse of components means they can be very efficient.* Once the necessary components have been defined, then preparing a new circuit for diagnosis can be as easy as defining the new circuit in a CAD tool. This is much easier than defining complex state graphs and dependency graphs by hand.

Disadvantages of Component-Based Circuit Models without Faults

- *They only work well in some domains.* Electrical and hydraulic systems can be defined in terms of their components fairly easily. Some domains are much more challenging to represent in this way. Mechanical systems, for example, are often much harder to describe in terms of component behavior and structure.

- *They do not work well where a fault causes extra behavior.* Where a component failure causes functions not to occur in the circuit, then the dependencies give a good indication of what components are suspects. However, where the component failure causes extra behavior, then it can be harder to decide what failure might have caused the extra behavior. For example, a wire in the example circuit shorting to the battery might be difficult to diagnose using only a correct model of circuit behavior. In order to make a more exact diagnosis, models of faulty component behavior are needed.

5.1.4 Component-Based Circuit Model, with Fault Models

The description of a component can be enhanced by the addition of details of a component's behavior when it is faulty. This enhancement can enable a clearer description of the behavior of the system under failure conditions, and can improve the diagnostic usage of the model. There will need to be a separate description of component behavior for each class of failure.

For example, in the electrical example used throughout this section, fault models for the relay might be "stuck at open" (the relay switch does not close when the coil is powered) and "stuck at closed" (the relay switch is closed whether the coil is powered or not).

The component behavior description can be enhanced with an extra set of information that describes the fault modes of the component.

For each fault mode, the different internal component dependencies that operate under fault conditions must be described. For the relay, the correct dependencies were that when the state of the coil was Active (current is flowing through it), the value of the switch resistor was zero (the switch is closed), and when the state of the coil was Inactive (no current is flowing through it), the value of the switch resistor was infinite (the switch is open). For the relay stuck at open, the value of the switch resistor is infinite, no matter what the value of the coil resistor. For the relay stuck at closed, the value of the switch resistor is zero, no matter what the value of the coil resistor.

The correct version of a component can be replaced in a simulated circuit by a faulty version, and a state graph generated for the faulty version of the circuit. If Relay 1 was stuck at closed, then the state graph in Figure 5.5 would be generated.

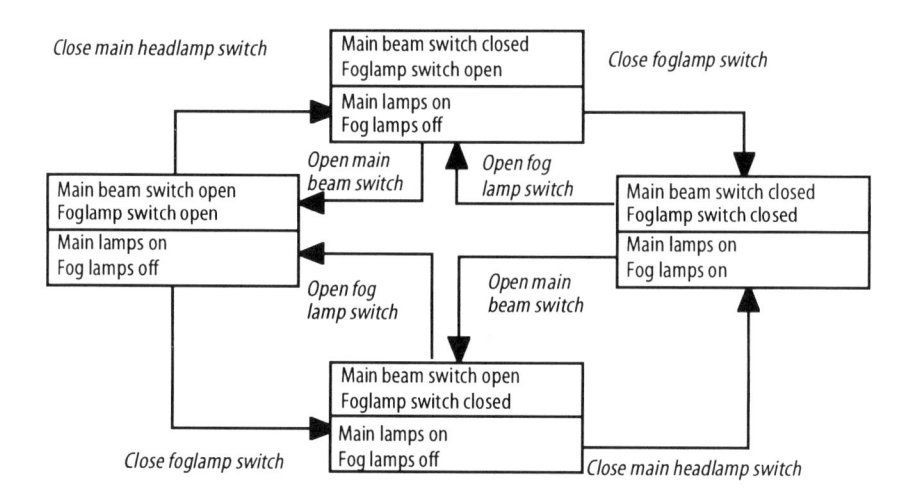

Fig. 5.5 State graph for circuit with relay stuck at closed.

The use of fault models of components to generate state graphs for faulty versions of circuits provides an alternative way of generating suspects for investigation. Instead of using dependency graphs in the way described in Section 5.1.1, state graphs of faulty behaviors can be used in the following algorithm:

Generate a state graph for the correct behavior of the circuit (as in Figure 5.3).

Use the correct state graph to prompt the user to describe the actual (faulty) behavior of the circuit (as described in Section 5.1.2, and illustrated in Figure 5.4).

For each possible fault model for each component in the circuit:

Replace the component with its faulty version.

Generate a state graph for the version of the circuit containing that faulty component (similar to the example in Figure 5.5).

Compare the state graph for the actual faulty behavior with the state graph for the circuit containing this fault model.
If the two state graphs match, then add this component with this fault to the list of suspects.

The list of suspects produced by this method can be more exact than the list of suspects produced using the dependency method. For the example where the right fog lamp is not working, fault models for splice S3 where some of the pins are still connected to each other would produce the extra possibility that the splice is faulty – mistakenly discarded by exoneration because the left fog lamp was still functioning correctly.

The suspects are also more specific. Wire W22 going open circuit would account for the failure behavior, but wire W22 shorting to ground would not account for it.

Having produced a list of suspects by this method, the detail of the simulation for the failed version of the circuit (the state of each of the components) can be used to generate tests to discriminate between the remaining suspects. For example, if Relay 1 had failed open, simulation of the circuit containing that fault would show that there would be current in wire W15 (through the coil of the relay), but not in wire W16 (through the switch of the relay). This information could be used to test for that failure.

Advantages of Component-Based Circuit Models with Fault Models

- *More exact simulation of faulty behavior.* The use of fault models for components gives improved simulation of faulty behavior. Without fault models, all that can be said is that the behavior of the faulty device does not match the correct behavior. With fault models, it is possible to say that the behavior of the faulty device does match specific failure behaviors.

- *More exact fault identification.* Without fault models, only dependencies within the simulation are available for deciding which components may be responsible. This tends to implicate many more candidates than when fault models are available.

- *Better test information.* Simulation with fault models provides better information on the failure state of all components in the device. This information can be used to discriminate between suspects.

Disadvantages of Component-Based Circuit Models with Fault Models

- *Component definition involves more work.* In order to be able to use fault models, it is necessary to identify all of the ways in which a component can fail. This involves a reasonable amount of work for electrical components: they tend to have a few significant failure types. More importantly, the common components are highly reusable, and so the work is well worth doing. This is not necessarily the case in other domains.

- *It is hard to cover all types of fault.* Components can fail in novel ways, and will not be correctly identified as the cause of the problem if the correct fault model does not exist. For this reason, some model-based diagnostic systems fall back on dependency-based fault identification if use of fault models fails to locate the cause of the problem.

5.2 Choosing which Aspects of the Domain to Model

The previous section considered different ways in which a system could be modeled for diagnosis. The component-based simulation models – with or without fault models for components – have significant advantages over the other choices. They have greater usefulness: they can be used to perform the same tasks as both the dependency models and the state-based models. They have much greater reuse: good components should be reusable to model new systems made from similar components. In order to use component-based simulation models for a particular application, there are two further decisions to make:

- What is a component in this application?
- What kind of granularity of simulation should be chosen?

The answers to these questions, which were used for illustrative purposes in the previous section, were that components mapped on to physical components in the circuit, and that the simulation was qualitative: only dealing with presence or absence of current in parts of the electrical circuit.

In other application domains, very different modeling choices may be appropriate. For example, models of a chemical processing plant might be based on the processes taking place rather than on the physical components of the plant. The same types of models discussed in the previous section can be used but it means that the term *compositional* modeling is more accurate than *component-based* modeling.

Similarly, for some electrical diagnostic applications, reasoning simply about the presence or absence of current would not be sufficient, and it might be necessary to construct more detailed models of the diagnostic domain in order to be able to perform diagnosis.

This section will consider the range of modeling choices and explain their advantages and drawbacks.

5.2.1 Goals for a Compositional Representation

Several different types of model are candidates for representation and reasoning in a domain. Consideration of what is needed from the representation enables the evaluation of different types of model by comparison with the identified requirements.

Ideally, useful compositional models for diagnosis should:

- *Reflect the device structure.* An obvious association between the physical components of an actual device and their representation in the model is important for diagnosis in many domains. Faults on devices are often caused by changes to the physical structure of the device being diagnosed. Therefore, in order to identify the cause, the model will need to relate to the structure as closely as possible. We have already observed that in some domains the physical structure might be less important than the processes occurring. In that case, it is the relationships between the processes that need to be reflected, not necessarily the relationships between physical components. It is worth noting that heuristic rule-based diagnostic systems of the type considered in Chapter 3 can have this characteristic of reflecting the device structure – they can be built in such a way that they associate symptoms directly with the structural faults that cause them – but they then fall down badly on the next characteristic.

- *Be reusable.* This is the ability to break models of devices down into fragments that can be used again when modeling other related devices. This capability is closely intertwined with the issue of mapping the model onto the structure of the device. Often, the reusable parts of models will parallel reusable components or processes in the domain (in the mechanical domain, for example, models of springs or connectors might be reusable in a wide variety of devices).

- *Be accessible.* In order to perform diagnosis, it must be possible to map the results of running the model onto what is happening in the real world fairly easily. In practice, this means reasoning symbolically in such a way that interpreting the analysis of the model is a straightforward task.

- *Be understandable.* This is not necessary in order for the representation to be useful for diagnosis. However, it will enable domain experts to build device representations more easily, make it simpler to explain the diagnostic results and will increase the acceptability of the results in the user community.

- *Be easily obtainable.* In many domains, design is done using CAD tools to describe the relationships between the components in the domain. Where that is the case, it is very helpful if the reusable components map onto the components being described in the CAD system.

Having identified the properties that are desired from a compositional representation, the alternative types of representation can be considered. Unfortunately, there is no single correct solution. The correct choice will depend on the domain and the type of diagnosis being done. Some guidelines are provided for when a particular representation might be appropriate, and Chapter 6 provides some example applications that should help to fill out what choices are made in practice.

5.2.2 Deciding on Components

Models of Physical Structure and Behavior

Work in this area was pioneered by de Kleer and Brown (1984) and by Davis (1984). This type of model is often applicable when devices can be described in terms of their components and the way in which the components are joined together (often the case with manmade systems).

The behavior of the component is described independently of any particular device. In practice, this means describing its behavior over a wide range of circumstances. The structure of the whole device is described – the components that comprise the device, and the ways in which those components are linked together – but not the behavior of the whole device. The overall device behavior is synthesized from the device structure and the behavior of the components.

When modeling faulty versions of a device for diagnosis, it is possible to specify failure modes for each type of component, or to just treat behavior of a component as unknown in the case where it is incorrect. Either way, incorrect behavior of the whole device can be obtained by simulating a device with a component or components with incorrect behavior.

There are several advantages in choosing to model the physical structure and behavior of a device:

- *High degree of modularity.* The behavioral description of each component can be encapsulated in a module. These modules are reusable in a variety of devices. Failure modes can also be related to these modules. In some domains, for example mechanical devices, the connections between components are so important to the behavior of the whole device that different types of connection are also best treated as modules of behavior.

- *Strong mapping to real device.* If the simulation is carefully based on device structure and component behavior, then it is possible to alter the structure or alter a component's behavior, and the device simulation will alter automatically to reflect those changes. This enables the identification of the faulty components responsible for the failure.

The ease with which the results of the simulation can be analyzed will depend to some extent on the level of granularity of the model, and this will be considered later.

The suitability of models of structure and behavior depends on the domain. This approach is not suitable for domains where behavior of the whole system cannot easily be synthesized from behavior of components. This means that reasoning about the behavior of gases, liquids or polystyrene beads in this way is not sensible.

Logical Models of Structure and Behavior

This is similar to the reasoning from structure and behavior described above, but here the structure used is the logical structure of the device, not the physical structure. It has been used successfully in electronic domains (Davis, 1984; Genesereth, 1984; Preist and Welham, 1990). The representation employed ignores the physical aspects of the circuits for the most part, and concentrates on the logical relationships between components implied by the connections. There can be additional problems, even for electronic applications, when physical structure is significant (for example, in bridging faults). Davis (1984) and Preist and Welham (1990) both attempt to overcome these problems by using information about physical structure in parallel with their logical model.

The advantages and drawbacks of the logical models are similar to those listed for physical models, except that the close mapping of the model is to the logical structure of the device not the physical structure. This is much more appropriate for electrical, hydraulic or pneumatic devices than it is for mechanical devices.

Process Models

Forbus (1990) has developed a language for describing the processes that occur in physical phenomena. It is able to describe such processes as liquid flow, boiling, evaporation, and cooling.

These processes are modular and can be linked in order to describe the behavior of a whole system. This type of modeling is useful for reasoning about systems where the processes happening in the system are its most important features. The behavior of a refrigerator, for example, could be described in terms of the processes just mentioned plus a few others.

Forbus has also done some excellent work on linking these modular descriptions of processes to quantitative simulation fragments (Forbus and Falkenhainer, 1990, 1992), and qualitative process modeling looks very promising for use in guiding the application of quantitative simulation. It is less clear that process modeling will be useful in practical diagnostic applications.

Where the fault to be identified is a fault with a process (e.g. cooling of a chemical reaction is not taking place), then this kind of model could be very helpful for problem identification and fault localization. It is of less help for fault identification and fault diagnosis – it cannot help in identifying the component responsible for the failure. For example, if cooling water was not being circulated because of a blocked cooling water pipe, then some kind of structural model would be needed to decide what structural changes might account for the process failure.

In summary, process models are useful and often necessary if the processes taking place in the domain are significant for diagnostic reasoning. However, they are not sufficient for allocating blame to components – for that, a model of structure and behavior would also be necessary.

Causal Models

This type of model is often the simplest to build for a single application. The behavior of the whole device is explicitly embedded in the representation. A seminal paper in this area (Rieger and Grinberg, 1978) gives examples of causal representations of a wide variety of devices – flush toilets, digital electronic circuits, and a child's toy called "the Marvelous Dipping Duck".

The flush toilet model embeds relationships like "the flow of water from the cistern to the toilet bowl causes an increase in the height of water in the bowl". In that particular example, the causal model is similar to the result of running a process model for the toilet, and includes both the type of information in the simple dependency models discussed in Section 5.1.1, and that in the state-based models discussed in Section 5.1.2.

Such models can be very useful for diagnostic and design purposes (see Sticklen, 1987; Pegah et al., 1993), but they suffer from the same problems for diagnosis as rule-based systems do. A causal description only of the correctly working device is not a sufficient foundation for model-based diagnosis. The model builder would need to enumerate explicitly all the possible faults that can occur to the whole device (and all possible states that it can be in for each fault). This is a lot more work than deciding on each failure that can happen to each type of reusable component. If the device is redesigned with a slightly different structure, then the whole model must be reappraised, and a new analysis performed by the diagnostic system designer to obtain the effects of all possible faults on the device.

While causal models are easy to build, they fail to meet the criteria outlined earlier of modularity and of direct mapping onto the physical structure of the device.

5.2.3 Choosing Level of Granularity

Quantitative versus Qualitative Models

As well as needing to decide what kinds of primitives make up the model-based representation, it is necessary to decide what kinds of values those primitives can take. For many engineers, the default choice is to use quantitative numerical values in the simulation.

One reason for this choice is that such models have often been developed during design, to ensure that the correct performance of the equipment meets the design requirements, and so simulation results for correct behavior can be easily obtained.

This is the basis of much of the work of the Fault Detection and Isolation (FDI) community (Patton et al., 1989). It is possible to use numerical models to predict the expected values of observed variables over time, and thus to detect when deviations from expected values occur due to faults. This kind of model-based monitoring is important for real-time systems, and is explored further in Chapter 7. It provides a good way of implementing problem identification, but gives little help for the other areas of diagnosis, where FDI researchers use other techniques such as rule-based systems.

There are several reasons why it is harder to use numerical models for fault localization and fault identification. One reason is that many such models are of the processes occurring in the domain, rather than component-based models, and so they have the same limitations as other process-based models, as discussed earlier in this chapter. A second reason limiting the diagnostic usefulness of numerical models is that exact values of parameters are no longer available when a fault occurs, and so it is not possible to perform simulations of failure situations. In practice, this means that where numerical models are used in diagnosis, they are only used for problem identification, and other methods are used to decide what to do about the problem that has been identified.

Qualitative models can complement the use of numerical simulation, as they are less effective at detecting that there is a problem, but better at assigning blame to specific components.

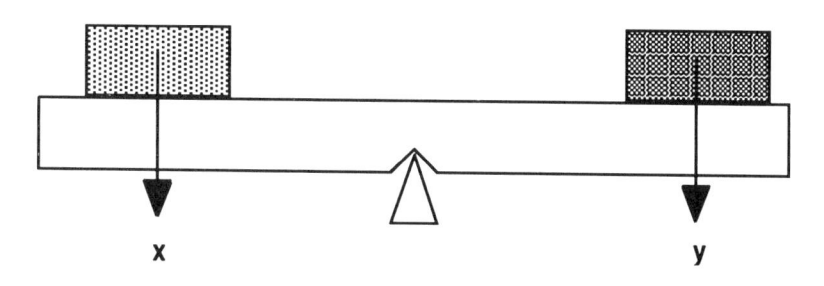

Fig. 5.6 Qualitative reasoning about weights on a balance.

Exact values are not necessary when reasoning about many everyday situations. For example, take the problem of deciding what happens with two weights, x and y, one each side of a balance, and the same distance from the pivot, as shown in Figure 5.6. It would be possible to calculate the answer for each possible pair of values of x and y. There are, however, only three possible outcomes, and they depend on whether the value x − y is less than, greater than, or equal to zero. Zero is a *threshold* or *landmark* value for x − y. Any other changes in the values of x and y will not affect the outcome. A change in outcome only occurs when x − y moves from a negative value to zero or from zero to a positive value. Qualitative reasoning involves identifying such critical values of variables as landmark values, and then combining qualitative values to determine the outcome of a situation.

Qualitative arithmetic and a qualitative calculus have been developed for combining and reasoning about qualitative variables that can only take the values +, − and 0. Cohn's survey article (1989) gives a reasonable introduction to the main strands of qualitative reasoning. As Cohn observes:

> "The crucial point about a qualitative quantity space is that it is a finite, discrete space which is much more amenable to reasoning about than the underlying continuous quantitative space. In particular, sets of equations can be solved by a finite number of guesses if required, and the number of possible states and behaviours is also finite (unless dynamic landmark creation is allowed)."

One of the great advantages of qualitative reasoning is that there are only a finite number of possible situations to investigate. This type of reasoning is also very useful when exact values are either not significant for the outcome of the simulation (as is the case in much failure mode effects analysis work) or not available (often the case in diagnosis). A related disadvantage is that the results of the simulation are often ambiguous.

The main advantages of the qualitative reasoning approach over a numerical simulation are:

- A qualitative simulation can be performed in cases where a numerical simulation would be impossible because of incomplete or only qualitative information being available in the domain. For example, reasoning about the effects of a leak in a pipe is possible, even though the amount of liquid lost is not known.
- A qualitative simulation can be performed much more rapidly than the comparable set of numerical simulations (covering the same set of values), and needs much less computing power. This is because of the comparative simplicity of the model.
- The symbolic representation of a qualitative model can closely match the structure of the device being modeled. This makes it easier for qualitative systems to produce explanations and justifications at an appropriate level for human comprehension than is the case with numerical models of a domain.

Identifying the Important Aspects for Diagnosis

After the decision has been taken to use qualitative modeling for diagnosis, there are still many choices that need to made. What aspects of the operation of the device need to be modeled? For example, when modeling an electromechanical device, is it necessary to model the fact that heat is generated in motors and in lamps. In many electromechanical devices, such effects are negligible, and would greatly increase the complexity of the modeling that was done. In other devices, to ignore such effects would mean that some kinds of common failure were ignored.

There is no magic solution to this problem. It is not feasible to model all possible aspects of a device, and so compromises have to be made. When deciding what aspects of a device to model, it is necessary to be aware of the compromises that are being made, and to identify the consequences of such compromises.

The first kind of compromise that is made is *abstraction* of the real device. Modeling the device in terms of its components, rather than its atoms is one level of abstraction. Another sensible abstraction is to model the device in terms of significant components. If the least replaceable unit is a subsystem, then there is no sense in modeling the device at the level of single components – no further information can be obtained than if the subsystems were the lowest level of modeling. Another strategy could be to model the device at different levels of abstraction, having a hierarchy of components, subsystems and systems making up the device. In theory, this should make the diagnosis more efficient, but in practice, hierarchical model-based diagnostic systems have not been very successful. It has proved more successful to implement the higher levels of the hierarchy in other ways (for example by dependency graphs), and only use compositional model-based reasoning for the lower levels of diagnosis. Abstraction might describe the behavior of the device at a more coarse level, but should always produce correct behavior.

A second kind of compromise that is carried out is *simplification* of the real device. Particular kinds of effects are ignored in order to make the simulation tractable. The example given earlier of ignoring heat effects in electromechanical devices is an example of simplification. The danger is that there are circumstances where simplification can produce incorrect results. When deciding on simplifying modeling choices, it makes sense to think about the kinds of fault that the models might not be able to simulate if such a modeling choice was made.

While no model will ever capture all of the minute detail of the device, the hope is that the chosen model will capture all of the significant detail. As Davis and Hamscher (1992) observe:

> "There will always be things about the device that the model does not capture. The good news is that the things the model fails to capture may have no pragmatic consequence. A schematic for a digital circuit will not indicate the color, smell or coefficient of friction of the plastic used to package the chips, but this typically doesn't matter. In theory, the model is always incomplete, and hence incorrect, in some respects, but it is a demonstration of the power and utility of engineering approximations that models are often pragmatically good enough."

5.3 Summary and Conclusions

Model-based diagnosis (MBD) uses models of a device or system as a basis for performing diagnosis. It is particularly effective when many different devices are composed of the same basic components, and those components are used as the modeling primitives. The components can be highly modular and give a good separation of the model from diagnostic reasoning. They can also be highly reusable for different devices.

Model-based reasoning has not been widely used for industrial applications in the past, possibly because it is a less accessible technology than rule-based systems or case-based reasoning systems. However, practical applications of model-based reasoning are beginning to emerge, and the next chapter explores three example applications where model-based reasoning is producing useful results. For domains such as automotive electrical systems, where many different devices are made from the same primitive components, it seems to be an ideal technology.

6. Applying Model-Based Diagnosis

This chapter considers some practical examples of model-based diagnostic systems. None of the systems discussed contains a perfect solution to the challenge of building efficient and effective diagnostic systems, but each one provides significant advantages over building a diagnostic system by manually constructing a diagnostic fault tree. Such advantages should be available in any application domain where the domain can be modeled, where diagnosis depends on the structure of the domain, and where the details of the structure are easily available.

6.1 RAZ'R from OCC'M

One of the main strands of research in model-based diagnosis has been in building a general diagnostic engine capable of performing diagnosis using constraint models of a domain. The most notable result of this research has been a tool called GDE (de Kleer and Williams, 1987). GDE was used by many researchers to experiment with model-based reasoning, and on the basis of this experience, several further tools have been developed that address some of the shortcomings of GDE.

GDE only used models of the correct behavior of components. As was explored in Section 5.1.3, this limitation restricts the information that is available for diagnosis. It is possible to identify which components might be responsible for absence of behavior. However, some components will be blamed spuriously. A standard example of where GDE gives odd results is where three bulbs are in parallel in an electrical circuit, and two of them fail to light. Two different explanations would be generated by GDE:

- the two bulbs that did not light have broken;
- the battery is broken and the bulb which is lit has failed in a mode where it spontaneously produces light.

Practically speaking, of course, the second possibility is most unlikely. Several extensions of GDE have been built to allow representation of the possible faults that can occur in a component, and to use that information in diagnosis. GDE+ (Struss and Dressler, 1992) is one example of a system that extended GDE to use representations of faulty components.

A German company called OCC'M has made a general diagnostic engine based on GDE+ available as a tool called RAZ'R. This section will describe RAZ'R in the context of an application to the anti-lock braking system (ABS) of a car. The ABS diagnostic example is documented in greater detail by Sachenbacher and Struss (1997).

6.1.1 The Technology

RAZ'R is a general purpose diagnostic tool – it can be used for diagnosing any problem for a device where the following items exist:

- a way of modeling devices such as the one under consideration;
- an appropriate structural model of the device;
- descriptions of the constraints between the components of the device.

The words "component" and "structure" are used very loosely here. Diagnosis using GDE and related systems has been used for such diverse problems as electrical devices, ecological systems, process control systems, and for detecting problems when tutoring students.

Because of the general applicability of RAZ'R, the first thing that must be done is to define an "ontology" for the specific application. Within RAZ'R, this involves defining the types of values that variables can take in components and the ways in which components can be connected.

In an electrical system with qualitative reasoning, the possible values for a resistance variable might be zero, load and infinity. Direction of a current might be characterized as having to take one of the three possible values $\{-, 0, +\}$.

If a model only had simple electrical connections, then any component could be connected to any terminal of any other component. However, RAZ'R could be used to model an electro-hydraulic system, and then it becomes necessary to define which types of terminal can be legally connected, to avoid the possibility of wrongly connected models, for instance where a pipe is connected to a battery rather than a fluid source.

Once the ontology for the application has been defined, it is necessary to use the ontology to develop models for each type of component in the device. The aspects of each component that need to be described are:

- terminals;
- parameters;
- state variables;
- structure;
- behavioral modes;
- behavioral details.

Terminals

These are the points at which the component can legally be connected to other components. They are similar in concept to the terminals described in Section 5.1.3. For pipes or wires, there would be a terminal of the appropriate type (hydraulic or electrical respectively) at each end. More complex components might have more connection points. A solenoid used to drive a hydraulic valve would have two electrical terminals, and two hydraulic terminals.

Parameters

These are constant values representing the behavior of an instance of a component type. For example, the resistance of the coil in an electrical relay, or the coil in a solenoid driving a hydraulic valve would each be constant. RAZ'R differentiates between values that are constant and values that can change (state variables are used for the latter).

State Variables

These are used to represent values that might change. So the resistance of the switch inside a relay would be a state variable, as it changes depending on whether there is current in the coil. Similarly for a solenoid used to drive a hydraulic valve, the resistance of the valve to fluid flow would change depending on whether the solenoid is energized or not.

Structure

RAZ'R allows the user to define aggregate component types as a number of simple components linked together. So an electrical relay might be defined as a resistor and a switch linked by a set of dependencies. The dependencies would be described in the behavioral details.

Behavioral Modes

This feature allows the user to list the possible types of behavior that this type of component can display. The default behavioral mode will tend to be OK. Other behavioral modes will describe the different kinds of failure behavior that the component can display. So a relay, for example, can fail stuck at open or stuck at closed.

Behavioral Details

For each behavioral mode, there will be a definition of how this component behaves. In RAZ'R, behavior is described in terms of constraints between the terminals. Constraints can be dependent on the operating state of the component – so the relay will have different constraints depending on whether the coil is energized or not. An example of the type of constraint expressions produced for a complex component is given in Figure 6.1.

Mode Variable Name	Variable Type
Diff	qP
DeltaDiff	qDeltaP
Mult1	qDeltaQ
Mult2	qDeltaQ

Behavior Description
A = + IF Cmd.command = true
A = 0 IF Cmd.command = false
DeltaA = 0 IF Cmd.command = true
Cmd.command = true IF A = + AND DeltaA = 0
DeltaA = 0 IF Cmd.command = false
T1.P = T2.P + Diff
T1.Q = - T2.Q
T1.Q = 0 IF A = 0
T1.Q = 0 IF Diff = 0
T1.Q = + IF A = + AND Diff = +
T1.Q = - IF A = + AND Diff = -
T1.Q = - IF A = - AND Diff = +
T1.Q = + IF A = - AND Diff = -
T1.DeltaP = T2.DeltaP + DeltaDiff
T1.DeltaQ = - T2.DeltaQ

Fig. 6.1 A behavior description for a complex component.

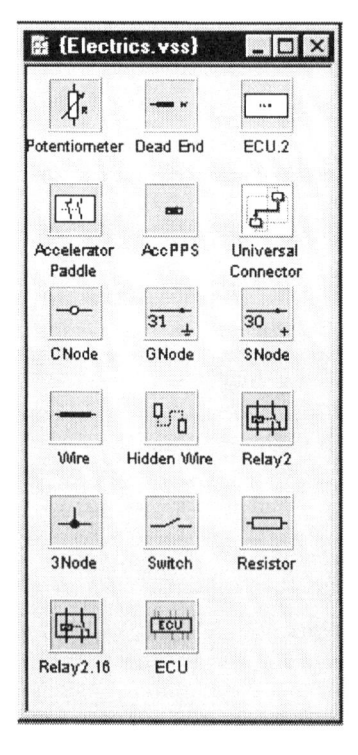

Fig. 6.2 An example component library.

Components will also have a graphical representation, including connection points representing the different terminals of the component. All of the component descriptions are held in a component library. When using RAZ'R to build a diagnostic application, you can select items from the component library to build a model of the device. The drawing package VISIO is used to provide structure building capability to RAZ'R. Figure 6.2 shows an example component model library.

The user can select components from the library by clicking the mouse on the wanted component type, then clicking on the structural drawing in the appropriate place. Connectors can be used to join the terminals of components together. In essence, the user can graphically build a description of the structure of the device to be diagnosed. The structure of the device includes the connectivity of the device, and the types of components that make up the device. Descriptions of the components already exist in the component library, and so the behavior of each component is already known, meaning that all of the information needed to simulate the device is available.

In order to use the device model for diagnosis, it is necessary to be able to describe the symptoms to be diagnosed. Possible symptoms are obtained by studying available information about the device (such as FMEA reports). Each symptom needs to be explained as a set of values of the model. When the diagnostic system is run, and the user chooses the symptoms of the problem, the RAZ'R diagnostic system searches for diagnostic candidates that produce behavior consistent with the anomalous readings corresponding to the symptoms.

The modeling and diagnosis procedure within RAZ'R will now be explained in greater detail in the context of the ABS application.

6.1.2 The ABS Application

The anti-lock braking system (ABS) is an electronically controlled hydraulic system. It provides computer controlled prevention of wheel lock-up or loss of traction if the driver brakes too strongly. Figure 6.3 shows the structure of the ABS device built within RAZ'R using defined hydraulic components.

In fact, to simplify the example, this is half of the ABS system. The braking systems are cross coupled, with the front left wheel and rear right wheel joined together as shown. The full system would also include the front right wheel and the rear left wheel, along with all of the pipe work for supplying hydraulic fluid to brakes on those wheels. The components used in the circuit are:

- four valves;
- two brake cylinders;
- a return pump element;
- an accumulator chamber;
- a throttle and damper.

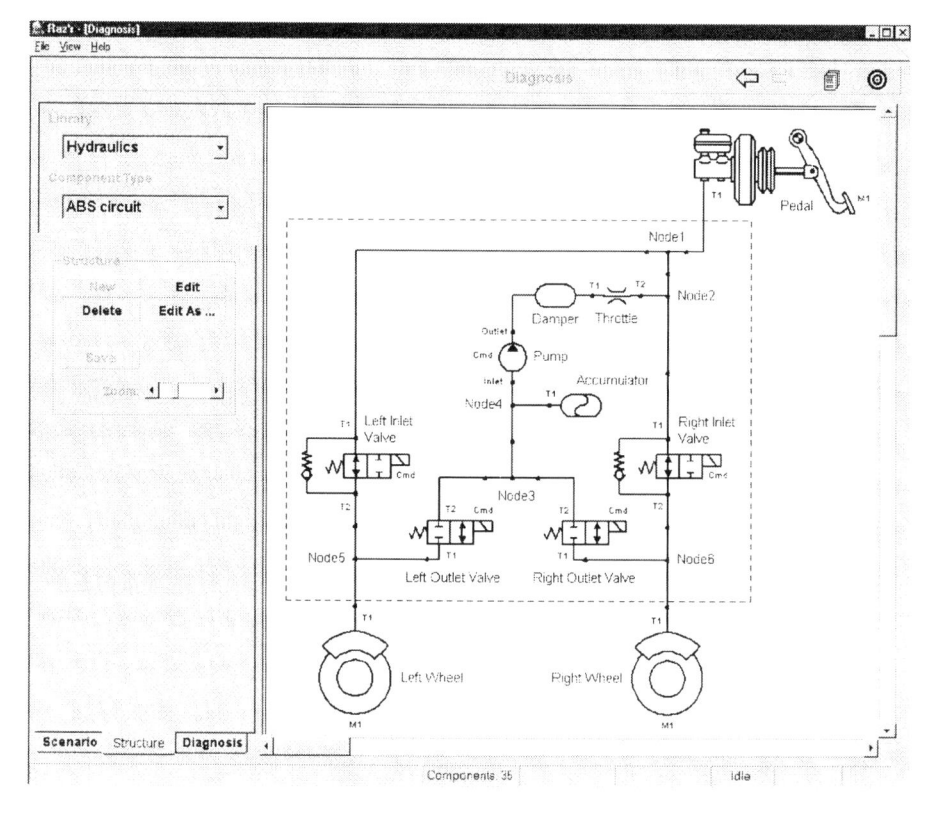

Fig. 6.3 ABS model within RAZ'R.

The valves can be controlled by the computer to vary the braking at each wheel in response to outside conditions. When the ABS goes wrong, there are several reasons why diagnosis of the ABS is difficult. Typical problems with the ABS are fairly badly specified, in user-level terms: "the vehicle is veering to the right", or "the left side of the car is braking too hard". The ABS system has no on-board sensing of pressure values, so it is not possible to improve the problem description by using actual values from the vehicle. It is also impossible to predict the precise dynamic behavior of the ABS, because it depends on unknown context conditions (such as how slippery the road surface is).

Because of the vagueness of the symptoms that can be provided and the unknown context where the problem occurs, qualitative descriptions of the problem and qualitative modeling of the ABS are appropriate for attempting diagnosis of this kind of failure.

RAZ'R uses the term "scenario" to refer to the symptoms that the user can identify as occurring. A separate scenario is constructed for each kind of problem that can happen, and is associated with the model of the ABS. For each scenario, the values of significant variables in the model in that scenario are described. The example shown in Figure 6.4 describes the state of variables in the circuit for the scenario where the car is yawing to the right side when braking. When the user says that

Applying Model-Based Diagnosis

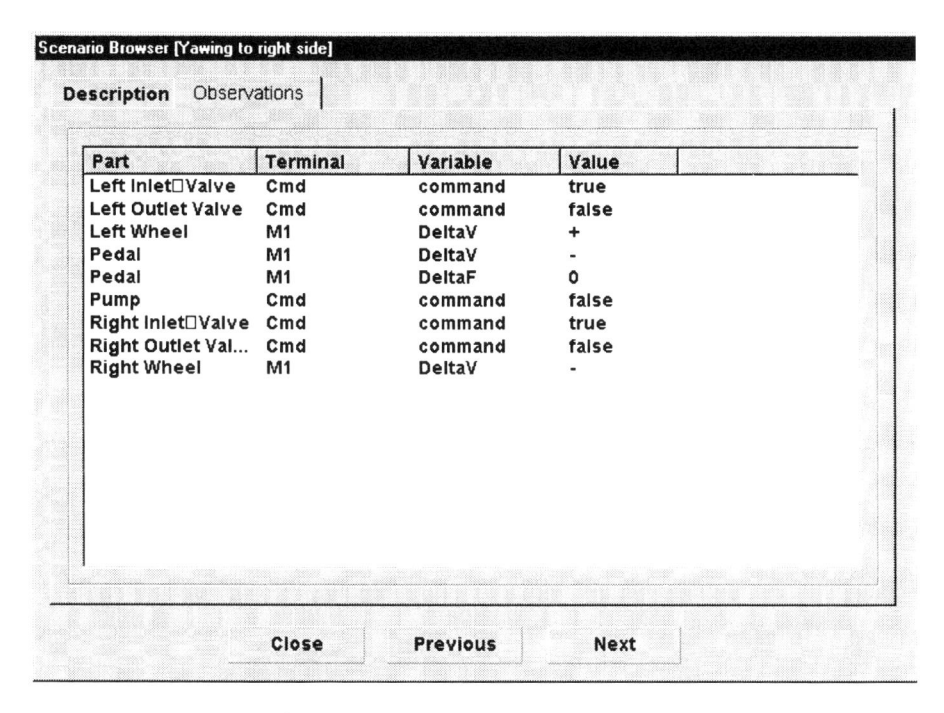

Part	Terminal	Variable	Value
Left Inlet☐Valve	Cmd	command	true
Left Outlet Valve	Cmd	command	false
Left Wheel	M1	DeltaV	+
Pedal	M1	DeltaV	-
Pedal	M1	DeltaF	0
Pump	Cmd	command	false
Right Inlet☐Valve	Cmd	command	true
Right Outlet Val...	Cmd	command	false
Right Wheel	M1	DeltaV	-

Fig. 6.4 Description of a typical problem in RAZ'R.

this scenario has happened, RAZ'R then translates that high-level description into the declared set of observed values.

The explanation of what this scenario means is: the command terminals on valves are the signals telling the valves whether to be open or closed, and *true* means that the valve should be open. Therefore, in this scenario, the left inlet and right inlet valves are supposed to be open, and the left outlet valve and right outlet valve closed (i.e. the car is supposed to be braking). *Delta* variables are so named because they describe changes rather than absolute values. The force on the pedal is constant (DeltaF = 0), and the pedal is moving downwards (DeltaV = -). The left wheel speed is increasing (DeltaV = +) and the right wheel speed is decreasing (DeltaV = -), which is what gives the overall effect of yawing.

RAZ'R calculates which components could cause this scenario to happen if they failed, and generates a list of suspect faults. The list of suspect faults can then be used as a basis to test which of the possible faults actually caused the failure.

6.1.3 Advantages and Disadvantages of this Approach

Advantages

- *It allows quick construction of diagnostic systems for variants of devices.* For companies building many devices that are essentially variants of each other, model-based diagnosis is a very efficient technology. This is relevant in many industries, including the automotive, aeronautic, and white goods industries. RAZ'R provides good tools for building reusable components for a model library, and for building models from a component library.

- *It can cover all possible failure combinations.* The GDE technology on which RAZ'R is based can identify possible faulty components even in the absence of fault models for components. This can be useful for identifying components that have failed in unexpected ways. RAZ'R is also good at identifying combinations of failures.

- *It can be applied in different kinds of devices.* The modeling in RAZ'R is based on propagation of local constraints, and many different kinds of systems can be represented in this way. Unlike AutoSteve, described in the next section, RAZ'R is not limited to electrical systems, but can represent devices that incorporate several different ontologies (electromechanical, for example).

Disadvantages

- *Constructing an ontology and a component library is difficult.* The general applicability of RAZ'R means that it is useful for many different kinds of diagnostic system. However, it also means that quite a lot of work needs to be done before it can be used for a specific kind of application. It is necessary to decide what to model for that kind of application, and how to model it. If you are building devices for a domain where someone has already created an ontology and a relevant component library, then it can be very easy to build diagnostic systems for new devices.

- *Diagnostic investigation is not necessarily efficient.* When performing diagnosis, RAZ'R produces a list of the most likely suspects that would account for the system. It does not help the user by providing the most efficient ordering for investigating the possibilities (as would be the case if the user was running a diagnostic fault tree type of program). If the user just tried each possibility on the list in the order given, then the diagnosis is likely to be very inefficient. Further programming would be needed if the user wanted RAZ'R to provide an efficient ordering for investigation.

6.2 Automotive Diagnosis from Design Models

6.2.1 Introduction

Failure Mode and Effects Analysis (FMEA) is a design discipline involving the examination at design time of the consequences of potential component failures on the functionality of a system. Usually, an engineer or group of engineers considers and then documents the effects of each (single point) failure on the operation of a system. The purpose of the analysis is to highlight any problems with a design and, if possible, to change the design to avoid significant problems.

Intuitively, the results of such an exercise should be useful for diagnosis, because they provide a mapping from the failure causes to the effects or symptoms. It should be possible to rearrange the results of the FMEA process to bring together all of the causes for a particular set of symptoms. A fault tree could then be generated automatically from that information.

In practice, FMEA reports are only used as a source of ideas for the kinds of faults that could occur, because they are not usually consistent enough for use in automatic generation of diagnostic systems. An engineer might write down different descriptions for different occurrences of exactly the same effect, or the same description for two slightly different effects. This lack of consistency makes it difficult to identify all of the failures that could manifest a particular set of fault symptoms, and so it is not easy to use the FMEA information in a diagnostic investigation.

Model-based reasoning can be used to generate an automated FMEA report. The far greater consistency of the automated FMEA report means that it has the right format to be used in building diagnostic systems. The fact that the information is generated at design time provides some assurance of its correctness, and also saves a great deal of time in building a diagnostic tree.

6.2.2 Automating FMEA

AutoSteve, (Price, 1998) a model-based system for performing automated FMEA, is in regular use at several automotive manufacturers and generates textual FMEA reports that are comparable with those produced by an engineer without automated help. Its major benefit as a design tool is that it significantly reduces the engineer time needed to perform an FMEA analysis, turning a task that might have taken an engineer several months into one that can be performed within a day. This makes it possible to perform an FMEA much earlier in the design lifecycle while design changes are comparatively cheap to make. Repeated analysis of a changed design using such a tool has even higher levels of time saving (Price, 1996). Secondary benefits are the completeness and consistency of the analysis that is performed.

AutoSteve employs qualitative model-based reasoning on electrical circuits combined with knowledge of intended system functions in order to generate electrical FMEA reports. It imports circuits directly from electrical CAD tools and generates a textual report on the effects of each failure mode. The report includes estimates of the severity, likelihood of detection and likelihood of occurrence for a particular failure.

AutoSteve has been integrated with TransCable, a commercially available electrical CAD tool. The circuit designer draws a design for an automotive subsystem using TransCable. From within the CAD tool, the circuit designer can verify the behavior of the circuit model by changing the state of switches and sensors, and can then request that AutoSteve generates an FMEA report. The designer is then expected to examine the FMEA report, noting significant effects and deciding whether improvements to the design are needed in order to improve safety or reliability.

The model-based reasoning underlying the AutoSteve system is a component-based electrical qualitative simulator with fault models, very similar to that described in Section 5.1.4. AutoSteve has definitions for common components and can be extended further by defining the qualitative behavior of new components, including how the component behaves under its possible failure modes. This can be done by the engineer using a graphical tool for defining the behavior of a novel component.

One complication of the scheme that was described in Section 5.1.4 is that the output of the simulator is too verbose for use in an FMEA report. The designer is only interested in the global effect of a failure, whereas the simulator generates results that include the state of every component in the circuit after every state change. For a circuit with 50 components and 20 possible state changes, that would mean a report containing 1000 pieces of information for each component failure. If there are 200 component failures, then the designer would be looking at 200,000 pieces of information. It would be difficult to extract significant information among all of the noise.

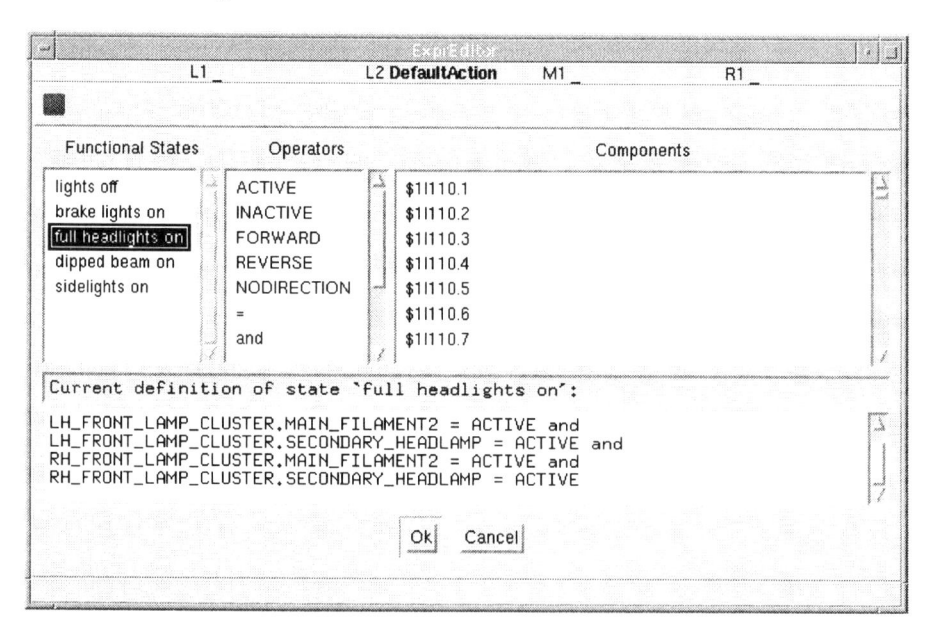

Fig. 6.5 Functional States Expression Editor.

In order to produce meaningful FMEA reports, functional states are employed to interpret the results of the qualitative reasoning. Figure 6.5 shows the tool that an engineer uses to describe how AutoSteve can identify when a function is being achieved. This example is for a simple lighting circuit (brake lights, headlights, parking lights). At the bottom of the window is the definition of four component states that need to be ACTIVE for the full_headlights_on function to be achieved. Functional states are reusable between different designs for the same automobile subsystem. When building a new design for an existing subsystem, the designer only needs to check that the existing functions are appropriate for the new design, and add any extra functions that are needed.

When the engineer has designed the circuit and linked it to the functional states, the AutoSteve system performs automated generation of an FMEA report in the following way:

- *Obtain the correct behavior.* Simulate the circuit through its possible changes, by operating the switches and changing the sensor states. The resultant behavior of the circuit is abstracted by recognizing when the operation of functions occurs (e.g. that when the headlight switch is closed, the headlight function and the license light function operate).

- *Make a list of failures that can occur in the circuit.* Possible failure modes are defined for each type of component. The complete list of possible component failures for the circuit can be compiled from the possible failures of each component in the circuit.

- *Obtain faulty behavior of the circuit.* For each possible single point failure of the circuit, impose that failure upon the circuit. Repeat the simulation and abstraction work that was done for the correct circuit and note the results.

- *Compare the faulty and correct abstracted behavior.* Functions that occur when they should not, or which do not occur when they should, describe the significant incorrect behavior of the circuit for a fault. Discrepancies of this kind can be used to generate a textual report for the effects of the failure. An extract from a report is shown in Figure 6.6.

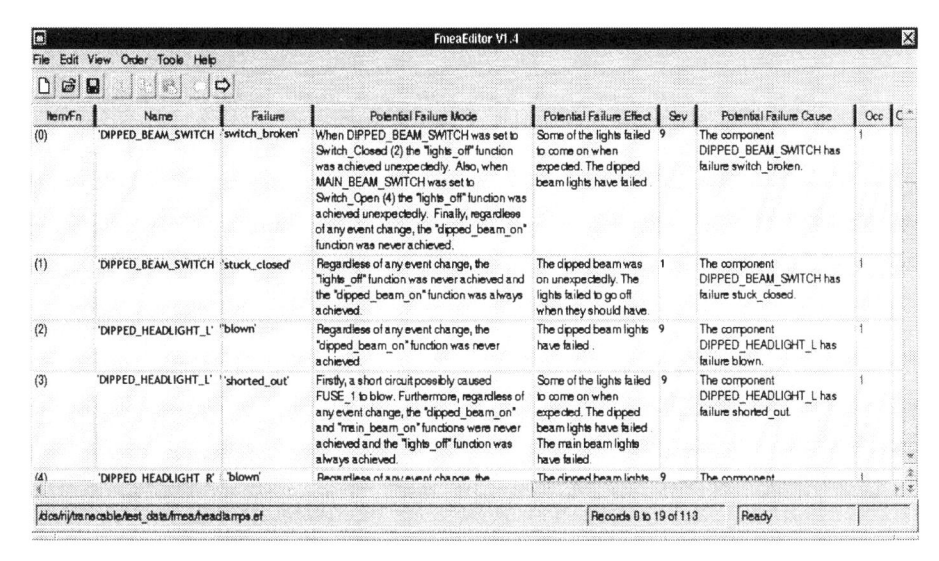

Item/Fn	Name	Failure	Potential Failure Mode	Potential Failure Effect	Sev	Potential Failure Cause	Occ	C
(0)	'DIPPED_BEAM_SWITCH'	'switch_broken'	When DIPPED_BEAM_SWITCH was set to Switch_Closed (2) the "lights_off" function was achieved unexpectedly. Also, when MAIN_BEAM_SWITCH was set to Switch_Open (4) the "lights_off" function was achieved unexpectedly. Finally, regardless of any event change, the "dipped_beam_on" function was never achieved.	Some of the lights failed to come on when expected. The dipped beam lights have failed	9	The component DIPPED_BEAM_SWITCH has failure switch_broken.	1	
(1)	'DIPPED_BEAM_SWITCH'	'stuck_closed'	Regardless of any event change, the "lights_off" function was never achieved and the "dipped_beam_on" function was always achieved.	The dipped beam was on unexpectedly. The lights failed to go off when they should have.	1	The component DIPPED_BEAM_SWITCH has failure stuck_closed.	1	
(2)	'DIPPED_HEADLIGHT_L'	'blown'	Regardless of any event change, the "dipped_beam_on" function was never achieved.	The dipped beam lights have failed.	9	The component DIPPED_HEADLIGHT_L has failure blown.	1	
(3)	'DIPPED_HEADLIGHT_L'	'shorted_out'	Firstly, a short circuit possibly caused FUSE_1 to blow. Furthermore, regardless of any event change, the "dipped_beam_on" and "main_beam_on" functions were never achieved and the "lights_off" function was always achieved.	Some of the lights failed to come on when expected. The dipped beam lights have failed. The main beam lights have failed.	9	The component DIPPED_HEADLIGHT_L has failure shorted_out.	1	
(4)	'DIPPED_HEADLIGHT_R'	'blown'	Regardless of any event change, the...	The dipped beam lights...	9	The component...	1	

Fig. 6.6 Example FMEA results.

For a typical car exterior lighting system, AutoSteve examined 214 single failures on 90 components, taking less than a minute to complete on an UltraSparc computer. A designer can use AutoSteve to produce an FMEA report for a system of this complexity within a day, where it might have taken several weeks to produce by hand. Much of the designer's effort is employed collating the circuit information, and with examining the results of the automatically generated FMEA report.

Unlike human-performed FMEA, AutoSteve is also capable of generating effects for multiple failures efficiently (Price and Taylor, 1997) and the multiple failure FMEA information can then be used to generate a diagnostic system capable of dealing with multiple failures. It can generate many thousands of failure combinations and has a method of pruning the failure reports so that the designer is only presented with the significant reports.

6.2.3 Generating Fault Trees

An FMEA report provides low-level links between failures and symptoms that are very useful for detailed fault identification within a single car subsystem. However, FMEA reports are generated for each major electrical subsystem in a car, and so this strategy can be extended to form the basis for a diagnostic scheme covering the whole of the car electrical system.

The top level program identifies the subsystem or subsystems that are causing the problem, giving some degree of fault localization. Figure 6.7 shows the top level of an example diagnostic system generated using FMEA output. It shows the set of car subsystems that can be selected, available from knowledge of what system FMEA reports have been generated. It facilitates fault localization on the basis of the subsystem where the problem is (exterior lights in this case).

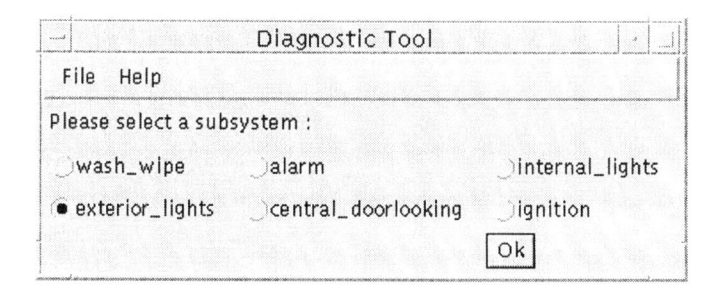

Fig. 6.7 Selecting a subsystem.

Next, the set of functions within the chosen subsystem is shown to the user for indication of which symptoms are present. A significant advantage of using AutoSteve FMEA reports as input to a diagnostic system is that the effect descriptions in the reports are based on the unexpected presence or absence of the intended functions of the design being analyzed. This means that the functions can be used to elicit a user-level description of the problem. In the car lighting circuit, for example, the intended functions of the circuit are at the level of user-identifiable symptoms (full headlights on, sidelights on etc.).

Figure 6.8 shows the set of functions listed for the exterior lights subsystem. Selecting the functions which have either failed or have occurred unexpectedly provides detailed fault identification. Information about which functions operate as expected can then be used to exonerate many suspects and to focus on the suspects that fit the user's description.

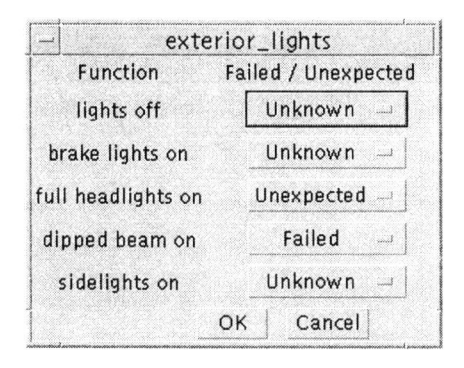

exterior_lights	
Function	Failed / Unexpected
lights off	Unknown
brake lights on	Unknown
full headlights on	Unexpected
dipped beam on	Failed
sidelights on	Unknown
OK	Cancel

Fig. 6.8 Identifying function differences.

Next, the diagnostic system determines a list of component-level suspects for the given fault signature, ordered by likelihood. The automated FMEA report contains failure mode and effect descriptions of the type shown in Figure 6.6. For each combination of component failures, we can determine the effect it has on the system in terms of its function differences (functions that failed to occur and functions that occurred unexpectedly). The descriptions are consistent: whenever the same set of symptoms occur, the description of those symptoms will match exactly. From such information it is possible to identify all failures listed in the FMEA report that have the same effect (e.g. all failures which can cause the car's dipped beams to not light when they should, or all failures which cause both the main beams and the dipped beams to be lit when they should not be).

After exoneration, the remaining suspects can be ordered by likelihood of occurrence (available from the FMEA report). No pair of failures in this circuit is more likely than any single failure, so in practice this will place the single failures at the head of the suspect list. The suspect list can be provided to the user as is illustrated in Figure 6.9.

An apparent exception to the heuristic that multiple faults are less likely to occur than single faults is the case of dependent faults, where one failure causes another (e.g. a short circuit often causes a blown fuse). However, AutoSteve computes the consequences of each failure during its simulation (e.g. it would detect that the short circuit had caused a fuse to blow and record any effects this had on the system functions). As a result, dependent fault cases are covered by the relevant single fault suspects and will be dealt with as single failure (high probability) suspects.

Once the failure has been localized using information about function, tests can be used to discover whether the most likely suspect is the actual fault. For example, if high beam relay stuck open is the most likely suspect, then testing the high beam relay will either blame or exonerate it. If high beam relay is not stuck open, then all multiple failure suspects that include that failure can also be deleted. In this way, the remaining possibilities can be addressed in a reasonable manner, and can be quickly pruned to select the right solution.

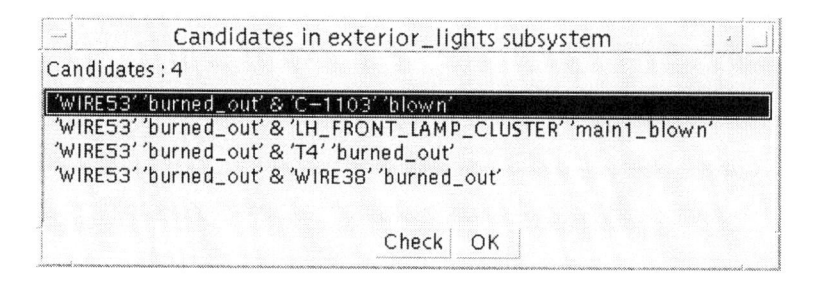

```
Candidates in exterior_lights subsystem
Candidates : 4
'WIRE53' 'burned_out' & 'C-1103' 'blown'
'WIRE53' 'burned_out' & 'LH_FRONT_LAMP_CLUSTER' 'main1_blown'
'WIRE53' 'burned_out' & 'T4' 'burned_out'
'WIRE53' 'burned_out' & 'WIRE38' 'burned_out'
                                          Check   OK
```

Fig. 6.9 List of suspects.

This section has described a separate diagnostic tool built to use the results of an automated FMEA. However, a more sensible choice might be to integrate the use of automated FMEA information into an existing tool for generating diagnostic trees. So, for example, diagnostic trees for use within GRADE (see Section 3.3) can be built from the FMEA information, and allow such information to be used without changing the development process that is currently followed.

6.2.4 Advantages and Disadvantages of this Approach

Advantages

- *Many more possibilities can be covered.* Compared with hand-generated diagnostic fault trees, it is possible to cover possible failures more comprehensively. Large numbers of the likeliest multiple failures can be added to the tree – many more than could be generated by a human building the tree, or from a human-generated FMEA report. The manual FMEA process is very time consuming, with the consequence that the engineer can only deal with single point failures. Automation of the electrical FMEA process facilitates information reuse for diagnosis by providing consistent descriptions of failure effects, and by speeding up the FMEA process to such an extent that it becomes feasible to examine multiple failures.

- *It fits into existing diagnostic processes.* Generating suspects at run-time, as RAZ'R does, is inefficient and demands a completely different diagnostic process from using tools to build fault trees. Using the scheme outlined here means that the suspects generated can be incorporated into existing practices.

- *It is a very efficient scheme.* By constructing the suspects from verified FMEA output, the method described in this paper generates suspects whose behavior has been examined by an engineer. This minimizes model-building effort, and gives a much higher degree of confidence in using model-based reasoning. The fact that the FMEA report has been checked by an engineer when the circuit was designed is attractive for diagnosis, as it means that the model-based information has undergone a degree of verification by engineers.

- *Diagnostic feedback to designers.* The FMEA output can be used in two ways to show designers the diagnostic consequences of their design decisions. The first is just to show them the diagnostic tree generated from their design. A more effective method of feedback would be to analyze the diagnosability of each potential failure and automatically identify sets of failures that are difficult to distinguish between. A diagnosability report could then be produced for the designer to examine.

Disadvantages

- *It does not cover all failure combinations.* An advantage of run-time generation of failures, as done by RAZ'R, is that all possible failure combinations can be covered. The scheme outlined here only generates failures to a given level of likelihood, so there is the potential for missing some less likely failure combinations. In practice, this is not an important issue. Most hand-generated diagnostic trees only cover single failures, and so this scheme is a great improvement on that situation. Also, if the likelihood threshold is set so that all pairs of failures are included, then in order to not have a failure combination covered, at least three separate failures must be included. In most cases, the earlier failures should have been fixed before a third failure occurred.

- *The diagnostic system builders still need to improve the diagnostic fault trees.* As was explored in the last chapter, model-based suspect generation leaves a lot of work to be done, including ordering of the lowest level candidates for investigation. This scheme has helped, by careful pruning of suspects and by ordering them on likelihood. However, much more information about cost of tests would be needed for the lowest level ordering of candidates to be done correctly, and so that work is left to the person building the diagnostic system. Even so, the time taken to produce a diagnostic fault tree is much reduced by using the information from the AutoSteve tool.

6.3 Autonomous Spacecraft Diagnosis

When Apollo 13 encountered a problem with its air recirculation system, astronauts on-board the spaceship, along with many ground staff, put their minds to finding a creative solution to a challenging diagnostic situation. A successful resolution to the situation was possible because past space missions, unmanned as well as manned, have benefited from billion dollar funding, and flight operation teams consisting of hundreds of people. The New Millennium program, created by NASA in 1995, aims at cutting both the cost of missions and the size of the flight teams by an order of magnitude. At the same time, it intends to cut development time for new space probes. The New Millennium program creates much greater demands on diagnostic systems than was the case at the time of Apollo 13. For there to be successful recovery from unexpected problems in the future, it will be necessary to overcome the following obstacles:

- *No human presence on board.* All sensing and recovery actions will have to be done remotely.

- *Limited human intervention.* There are critical mission points, such as maneuvering into orbit around a planet, where a failure would need to be dealt with immediately. This means that the on-board diagnostic systems must have a degree of autonomy.

- *Greatly increased complexity.* Modern spacecraft (like modern automobiles) are much more complex, making it harder to take into consideration all of the things that might go wrong.

- *Multiple problems over time.* If the spacecraft is in space for a lengthy period, then several different crises will happen over time. The diagnostic system must be able to reason what to do in the context of reconfiguration that was done to address previous problems. This makes the number of possible problems and solutions to be considered far too large to be able to enumerate them all in a rule-based system.

The need to develop comprehensive autonomous diagnostic systems, and to achieve that goal at minimum cost, has caused NASA to turn to model-based reasoning for solutions, constructing a system called Livingstone (Williams and Nayak, 1996). Models are used in monitoring the state of the spacecraft systems, for diagnosis of problems encountered, and also for reasoning about the implications of reconfiguring the hardware to overcome problems. Model libraries have been developed in the kinds of ways that have already been described in Chapter 5 and earlier in Chapter 6, and with the same kinds of benefits:

- they provide reusable components;

- they reduce the time needed for implementing a new diagnostic system;

- they can spread the modeling costs across many related diagnostic applications.

In order to achieve all necessary aspects of planning and diagnosis, Livingstone is linked with HSTS, a planning/scheduling system, and RAPS, a system for executing plans.

An example application built using Livingstone was for a scaled-down version of Cassini, the most complex spacecraft built to date. A schematic for the engine subsystem of Cassini is shown in Figure 6.10. The kinds of component shown in the schematic are:

- *Valves.* These can be either open or closed (closed valves are depicted as solid black). It is possible to repeatedly move them from one state to the other.

- *Pyro valves.* These either start as closed or open. They can be opened or closed once only, and then fix in the changed position. They are more reliable than reusable valves, but take more power to operate.

- *Regulators.* These control the amount of fuel provided.

- *Tanks.* The containers of the propellant. The helium tank is used to pressurize the two propellant tanks (oxidizer and fuel).

- *Engines.* When the oxidizer and the fuel mix in the engine, they spontaneously ignite, producing thrust.

- *Pyro ladders.* These are series of pyro valves which can be used to change the state of the system a limited number of times, that is, blow the first pyro in the ladder to open the flow, and the second to close it, etc.

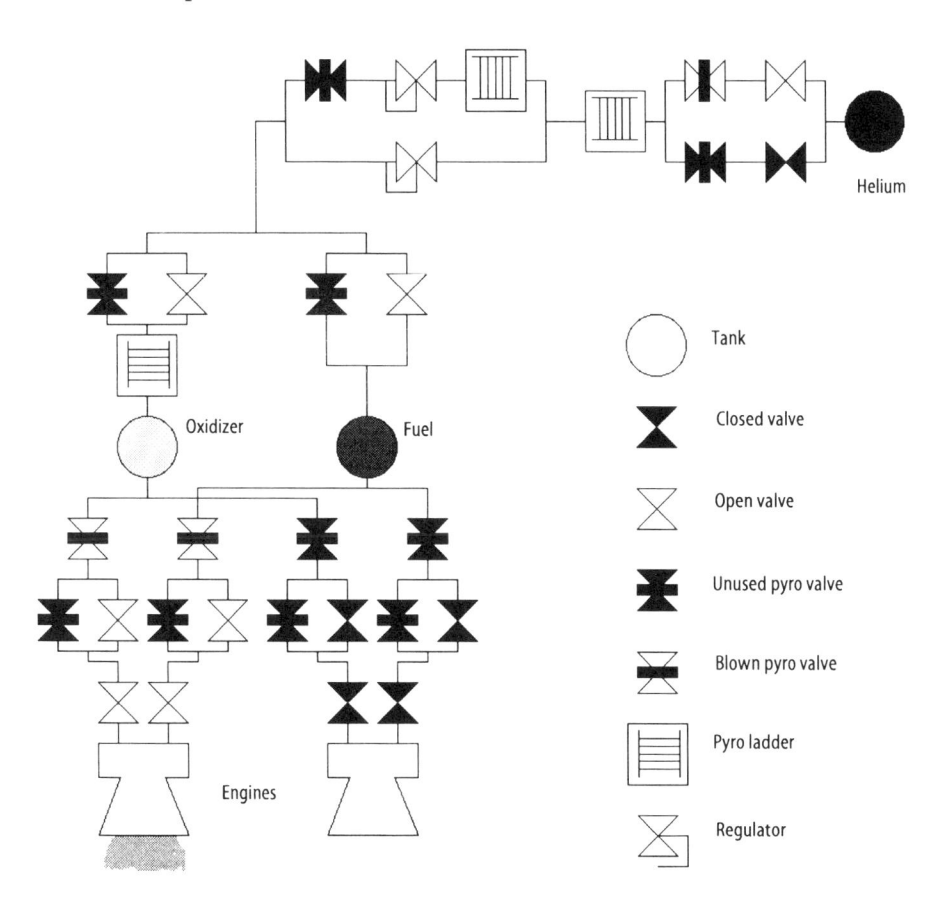

Fig. 6.10 Engine schematic for Cassini (taken from Williams and Nayak, 1996).

Component models are described as state transition models, with costs attached to the transitions to different states. They include transitions to failure states, with the transition to failure state annotated with the probability of the failure occurring. A component model for a valve is shown in Figure 6.11.

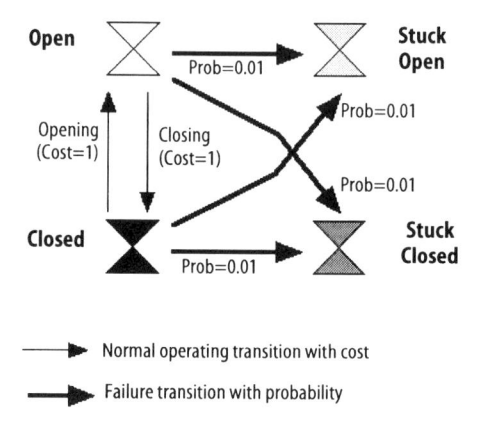

Fig. 6.11 Component model for a valve (taken from Williams and Nayak, 1996).

Models of the Cassini system are used for three stages of the operating process:

- *Mode identification.* This stage hypothesizes the most likely current state that the device is in (this can be the expected state, or an unexpected state, in which case diagnosis is performed).

- *Mode reconfiguration.* This stage generates the different series of component state changes that should lead to the desired state of the device.

- *Model-based reactive planning.* This stage chooses the best single component change to perform next and does it.

The three stages are repeatedly performed in order to reach a desired goal state. The repetition is done after a single component change rather than a series of component changes. If the previous mode identification was wrong, then the change of component state may reveal that before too many wrong actions have been taken.

For example, a set of valves must be opened in order to fire one of the spacecraft's engines (only one engine should be fired at any time). If the engine should fail to fire when all of the required valves have been correctly set, then mode identification will recognize that a valve has stuck closed somewhere. Mode reconfiguration can calculate sets of actions that will allow the other engine to fire instead. Model-based reactive planning will choose the least costly way of achieving the reconfiguration. Pyro valves are a limited resource, so solutions that change the minimum number of pyro valves will always be chosen.

The Cassini planning and diagnostic system built using the Livingstone model-based reasoner was tested on a challenging scenario. It was required to run a simulated autonomous insertion of Cassini into orbit around Saturn under different failure conditions. There was no communication with earth during the insertion period, the engines had been idle for several years (hence the different failures), and different maneuvers were needed in order to move through the plane of Saturn's rings.

The Livingstone-based planner and diagnostic system passed the test scenarios with flying colors, and has been selected as part of the core autonomy architecture of NASA's New Millennium space program.

Many of the advantages of Livingstone are shared with the two previous examples. However, a major difference is in the continuous nature of the way in which Livingstone operates. It is expected to be able to deal with an environment that changes over time, working in a continuous manner, and carrying out recovery actions in an autonomous manner. Compared with the other two systems discussed in this chapter, that means that it has a much higher emphasis on planning and taking actions. The model-based reasoning is only part of a larger system. Compared with other methods of building diagnostic systems, model-based reasoning provides perhaps the only feasible way of attaining the desired goals.

7. Real-Time Diagnostic Systems

Most of the diagnostic systems that have been described so far have been interactive and "single-shot" in nature. When a problem occurs, the diagnostic system prompts a user for the details of the problem, and suggests solutions. The diagnostic session is completed when the problem has been solved to the user's satisfaction, or when the diagnostic system has run out of possible solutions to the problem.

The diagnostic systems dealt with in this chapter are different. Instead of being prompted by user concern, a diagnostic session is usually prompted automatically, often due to continuous monitoring software detecting some kind of inconsistency. The information needed to perform fault localization and fault diagnosis is often available on-line. In some cases, the action taken to mend the fault can also be initiated automatically, but in other cases, it is enough that the fault has been identified and a human operator alerted.

Example real-time diagnostic problems addressed by the methods covered in this chapter include:

- on-board diagnostic systems in automobiles;
- detection of gas turbine problems;
- incipient fault detection and resolution in steel mills;
- helicopter gearbox failure detection;
- chemical process control plant diagnostic systems.

There are some shared characteristics of the diagnostic systems listed that place these applications into the same category. While not all of the characteristics will be shared by all the listed diagnostic systems, it seems helpful to start by considering the kinds of features that real-time diagnostic systems tend to have that other diagnostic systems usually do not have. Following that consideration, the chapter will describe techniques used to provide those features in implemented applications of real-time diagnostic systems.

7.1 Characteristics of Real-Time Diagnosis

7.1.1 Continuous Monitoring and Problem Identification

Whereas many diagnostic systems are in the context of a device which is already broken, one of the characteristics of most real-time diagnostic systems is that they have a strong emphasis on detecting problems as they develop, rather than waiting until a problem has become severe.

Helicopter gearbox monitoring is an excellent example of this. If you do not replace a helicopter gearbox until it has failed, then the helicopter will have crashed and you will have to replace the rest of the helicopter as well. Without condition monitoring, preventative maintenance would be done after every certain number of operating hours, irrespective of whether the particular gear box needed it or not. As well as sometimes being unnecessary, preventative maintenance is also very costly, both in terms of expensive components and labor, and in terms of expensive plant or equipment being unavailable while the preventative maintenance takes place. With effective monitoring, preventative maintenance can be reduced to when it is really needed.

Similar principles apply in many chemical process diagnostic systems. If there is an incipient problem with a chemical process, the sooner it is detected, then the sooner it can be corrected, and the amount of imperfect product produced will be minimized.

7.1.2 Changes in Monitoring Conditions

As rotating machinery gets older, vibrations from the machinery will change. In some cases, the changes are reasonable, and adaptation to the changes must be made. In other cases, the changes mean that the equipment is about to fail and drastic action must be taken. In order for condition monitoring to be effective, it must be possible to distinguish between the two different circumstances. This will often involve recording instrument readings over time, and being able to reason about data trends.

7.1.3 Hard Real-Time Constraints

This characteristic only exists in some real-time diagnostic systems. Some applications demand that action is guaranteed to be taken by a diagnostic system within a defined period. Where a process changes very slowly, the defined period might be several hours, and it is easy to guarantee a response within such a timeframe. Where a process can change very quickly, the defined period might only be seconds, or even milliseconds, and that is much more challenging to achieve. For example, an on-board automotive diagnostic system charged with detecting engine management problems might need to distinguish between several classes of fault very quickly. A sensor failure might mean that the engine can carry on working, although perhaps less efficiently. A loss of oil pressure, on the other hand, might mean that the engine should be shut down immediately in order to avoid engine damage. The diagnostic system must be able to distinguish between these two kinds of problems quickly enough to prevent engine damage.

7.1.4 Reasoning about Uncertainty and Time

Trends can only be discerned over time. When a problem starts to occur, the amount of relevant data will be small, and so the trend will be very uncertain. In order to act on the trend as soon as possible, it is useful to be able to assign likelihoods to possible problems, and then search (or wait) for further information that would confirm the trend.

7.1.5 Autonomous Decision Making

The car engine diagnostic problem mentioned earlier is a good example of where the diagnostic system needs to decide what immediate action to take without referring the decision to a human. The consequence of this is that the level of trustworthiness that the correct problem identification has been reached needs to be high.

The task of identifying that a problem exists is central enough to real-time diagnostic applications that it will be addressed in the next section, separately from the other steps in real-time diagnosis, which are more similar to off-line diagnosis.

7.2 Monitoring Real-Time Applications

There are several useful ways of building real-time monitoring and problem detection systems, and this section will discuss each of the following in turn:

- *Building monitors by hand.* They can be constructed as tests on sets of instrument readings.

- *Quantitative modeling.* For complex rotating machinery, a reasonable amount of success has been achieved with numerical models.

- *Qualitative model-based problem detection.* The Cassini system in Section 6.3 has shown that qualitative models can be used to detect inconsistent states in devices with many components and states.

- *Neural Networks.* These can be used either to model the device, or to provide a direct monitor.

For any of these methods, the prerequisite for developing a problem detection system is a representative set of logs of the system in operation. This should include logs of correct operation and logs of faulty operation. There are two difficulties with this. First, it can be difficult to decide even in hindsight, whether there is a fault at a particular point in time, where you are trying to detect an incipient fault as soon as possible. Secondly, it is not possible in all cases to collect data for all possible faults. For example, where a problem on a nuclear reactor would cause a melt-down, you would prefer not to try out that fault, although you would like to be able to detect it when it occurs.

Despite the problems with collecting logs of meaningful instrument readings, the logging phase is a vital part of most real-time diagnostic system projects. It provides test data for trying out the diagnostic system on realistic test cases. This is especially important for applications where failures are very rare, but very costly. Unplanned downtime on a steel mill is very costly, but is rare because of preventative maintenance. This means that a new diagnostic system on a mill might need to be installed for a year or two before a reasonable number of failures occurred. In order to test that the system could deal with failures, logged data is vital.

7.2.1 Building Monitors by Hand

If code is to be constructed to monitor for failures in a device, then a useful first step is to identify all of the ways in which the device can fail. The FMEA report on the device (if one exists) is a useful document at this point. It should provide a list of all of the component failures that could cause the device to fail. This might even be built into a diagnostic fault tree that would show how to decide what is broken in the situation where the device is allowed to proceed to complete failure. Such a fault tree would be useful in prompting experts to think of other failures not covered by the example fault tree.

Once a full list of possible failures has been made, then it is necessary to decide how each failure would manifest itself while failing. For some failures, such as sensors failing, there may be no sign of impending failure. In other cases, such as solenoids failing, or a fluid leak in the device, there may be characteristic signs that can be detected from instrument readings. Some of those characteristic signs may only be manifest in certain operating states of the device (e.g., certain incipient faults in a car braking system may only be indicated when braking is occurring, other incipient faults may only be indicated when braking is not occurring). There are also failures, such as some leaks, which can only be detected by keeping sets of readings over a time period, and observing a trend in the readings.

For each possible failure to be monitored, it will be necessary to list the following details:

- what the cause of the failure is;
- the test to identify whether the problem exists;
- data or data trend needed to identify that a problem has occurred;

- how often the test should be done (urgency of problem);
- operating state under which test should be done.

Several different failures may result in the same tests being done on the same set of data. This does not necessarily cause any problems. In the case of on-board car diagnostic systems for example, it is not always necessary for on-board diagnosis to identify the particular component responsible for the problem. It is often good enough to be able to classify the problem as either being of a nature to cause the engine to be stopped, or as a problem which will allow continued operation of the car, albeit at a reduced level of performance.

Such a diagnostic system is probably the best solution at present where a complex plant made up of many components is being diagnosed. A good example of such an application is a hot steel mill hydraulic plant. The hydraulic plant is too complex to model mathematically in any useful way for detecting incipient faults, while qualitative reasoning is not precise enough to detect the gradual development of a solenoid failure or a pressure sensor failure.

Because the monitors are set up to detect individual cases, then except where several different failures have the same overall failure behavior, the monitors will also provide discrimination between the different failures. As we have already observed, an imprecise diagnosis may not matter in many real-time systems, if the decision in all cases is the same (e.g. to replace a component during the next downtime, or to halt operation immediately).

Commercial toolkits have been built to help construct real-time diagnostic applications in the manner described here, and two of them are discussed in Section 7.4.

7.2.2 Quantitative Modeling

For complex rotating machinery, a reasonable amount of success in building monitoring systems has been achieved with numerical models. This approach works well where the device to be diagnosed is a single complex item, such as a turbine generator or a helicopter gearbox, and mathematical process models are available for the device. The full details of how this approach is implemented would fill a book on its own and is well documented in the literature (Frank, 1990; Isermann, 1993; Patton et al., 1989), but a brief summary will be provided here.

Given a set of measurements for a device, the mathematical models can be used to extract special features of the device. The way of extracting these features varies somewhat between the main methods (parameter estimation and observer-based methods), but essentially, a set of filtered residuals is calculated. These residuals can then be compared with the normal features of the correctly working process. Discrepancies between the two sets of feature values are symptoms of problems with the device.

Where correct mathematical process models are available, this approach seems to be a good way of detecting problems with large items of plant. It can have problems because of the unavoidable mismatch between the model and the real system, and where there is noise present. In addition, it often does not actually diagnose the cause of the problem, but just identifies that there is a problem of some kind. Because the residuals are transformed versions of the actual observed values, it can be impossible to link them to a particular input or output of the device. That often means falling back on rule-based methods to perform the main tasks of diagnosis once problem identification has been achieved using the quantitative models.

7.2.3 Qualitative Model-Based Problem Detection

Chapter 6, dealing with examples of qualitative model-based reasoning, contained two examples of systems that could be considered for real-time use.

Section 6.1 dealt with an off-board system for diagnosing car anti-lock braking systems (ABS). In that case, the user detected the problem and the diagnostic system used a model to identify components that could be responsible for the failure. The model used to perform diagnosis would not be capable of performing problem detection on-line. If the ABS provided on-line instrument readings of the different values in the qualitative model, there is no way of using this model to automatically detect problems such as over-braking on one wheel. The qualitative model does not provide the correct type of information for problem detection in this context. However, it does provide information on which values in the ABS can be expected to change when a particular fault occurs, and so can be used to calculate which readings are the most useful to observe, thereby helping to build a monitoring system of the kind described in Section 7.2.1.

Section 6.3 described a problem where qualitative reasoning has been used on-line for problem detection. The Livingstone system is able to detect problems in the Cassini propulsion system. However, the problems dealt with are ones where there is propulsion when no propulsion is expected, or vice versa. This can be detected with qualitative reasoning because a qualitative change of state has occurred. If the problem to be detected was a reduction in propulsion, then additional quantitative information would be needed.

Qualitative modeling usually comes into its own in the fault diagnosis phase of real-time diagnosis, and this will be explored more fully in Section 7.3.

7.2.4 Neural Networks

Neural networks have been used in two different ways for real-time problem detection. The first way is to train a net to detect the difference between correct and faulty behavior.

This can be done using logs of past failures. As long as there is sufficient information on-line to differentiate between different failures, then this approach can also be used to perform diagnosis. Where such logs are not available for all failures, it can be unwise to use this approach even for problem detection, as there is no guarantee that the net will be able to detect the new type of failure as a problem. Such information is not available for many safety critical systems, where it would be dangerous to deliberately induce faults on the plant in order to be able to observe and log problem data. One proposed solution to this (Hessel et al., 1997) is to use data from a simulator rather than real log data.

An imaginative way of using nets is to teach the net to reproduce correct behavior (Köppen-Seliger and Frank, 1996; Zhou and Bennett, 1997). The net can then be used to calculate the correct behavior, and residuals can be calculated in the same way as if a quantitative model was available for the system. This extends the quantitative method described in Section 7.2.4 to applications where no mathematical process model is available. The net provides the same results as a quantitative model would.

7.3 Diagnosing Real-Time Applications

Once monitoring has identified that a problem exists, it is necessary to decide what to do about the problem. Most of the diagnostic techniques discussed earlier in the book could come into play at this point. Case-based reasoning has not proven popular for real-time systems. This is possibly because a monitoring system may have already clustered potential problems so that when a problem is detected, it could only have one of a limited number of causes, and so the diagnostic problem is more focused than the kinds of problems usually dealt with by case-based reasoning. Another reason is that case-based diagnosis works most easily where a textual description of the problem is available, rather than a set of instrument readings.

Diagnostic fault trees and model-based reasoning can each be used to identify the cause of the particular problem. Where there are enough past cases, neural networks have proved quite popular. Neural networks and model-based reasoning share a problem for off-line diagnosis that does not exist for on-line, real-time diagnostic systems. If a user has to be asked for information, then neither technology works very well compared with a diagnostic fault tree, because of the need to ask the user for that information in a sensible order. That limitation is less of a problem for real-time diagnostic systems. If all the required information is available as on-line readings, then the diagnostic system can obtain it in whatever order is preferred, without having to bother the user.

7.3.1 Heuristic Work

Where the problem detection software is implemented as hand-built problem detection monitors, then in many cases the possible causes of the problem will also have been narrowed down to one or two possible causes, because of the specific nature of the tests carried out. Very little extra work will need to be done to identify the actual failure.

Table 7.1 gives an example of a monitoring rule written in the real-time tool COGSYS to detect problems on a steel mill. Some of the terms in the rule (such as NORMAL and SPIKES for the state of the mill presses) are generated by lower-level C monitoring code, which turns raw data into higher-level trends. There are a series of steel presses in the mill, and the hash sign before *press* in the rule means that the rule is applied to each of the presses in turn.

```
--- if any press is in servo mode or balance mode
--- and metal is entering or leaving mill stand
--- and new state is NOT normal
--- and time since metal change is > time when it should steady
--- then there is a problem with the corner.

--- If press is spiking or oscillating then don't know what it is,
--- but prompt other rules to find out...
--- else if it is offset from the normal value, pressure transducer
--- has offset problem.

    RULE PRB_stuck_in_metal_change

    IF #press.mon_servo_or_balance
    AND #press.fault = METAL_CHANGE
    AND (#press.new_state /= NORMAL)
    AND ((NOW() - #press.metal_in_time) > metal_dur)
    THEN
        IF #press.new_state = SPIKES OR
            #press.new_state = OSC_OR_SPIKES
        THEN
            #press.new_fault
            IS POS_OSC_OR_SPIKES CERTAINTY CERT_VALUE(0.5) \CUT;
        ELSE
            IF #press.new_state = OFFSET_VALUES OR
                #press.new_state = OFFSET_OR_SPIKES
            THEN
                #press.new_fault IS POS_OFFSET_VALUES
                    CERTAINTY CERT_VALUE(0.2) \CUT;
            ENDIF
        ENDIF
    ENDIF
```

Table 7.1 Monitoring COGSYS rule for steel mill.

Once a number of such rules have been run, then possible faults will be ordered by likelihood of occurrence, and any faults with a high level of likelihood can be notified to mill operators for attention.

Where the problem detection is carried out by quantitative modeling, then more work is needed to identify the specific failure. Often, the fault diagnosis part of the diagnostic system can be as much work as building a problem detection and diagnosis system by hand. The reason that quantitative models are used is that they give very good detection results for complex rotating machinery, and for that kind of application the best diagnostic system is achieved by having the quantitative model for problem detection and then implementing the rule-based fault diagnosis system to identify the cause. So, if a quantitative model was implemented for the steel mill, rules of the kind shown in Table 7.1 might still be necessary in order to decide why the mill readings were deviating from normal.

7.3.2 Neural Network-Based Diagnosis

Where examples of behavior for each possible failure are available, it is possible to train a net to decide on the cause of a problem as well as to detect that the problem exists. Kirkham and Harris (1997) give an example of a neural network being used for both problem detection and fault identification. This is achieved with two stages of network. The first stage networks are trained only on good data. When problem data is monitored by the first stage network, it is recognized as novel (and therefore a problem). The second stage networks are trained to associate the error distance from the correct behavior for a particular fault with that fault.

As we have already observed, this type of work assumes two things. First, it assumes that the first stage networks will correctly learn what discriminates good behavior from bad behavior. This is possible but there are dangers that what has been learned will not discriminate some classes of bad behavior. The second assumption is that example logs for all classes of error are available for the second stage network to learn the characteristics of that error. In fact, given the second assumption, the data for all of the error situations can be used both to train the first stage networks and to verify the first assumption. There are applications for which these assumptions apply.

This technology has been tried out on a Wiggins Teape paper mill. Published results were that the problem detection rate was unsatisfactory, but in all cases where the system was able to recognize that a problem existed, it was able to classify the fault correctly.

7.3.3 Qualitative Model-Based Work

The examples in Chapter 6 give a good idea of how qualitative models can be used to diagnose real-time systems once a problem has been detected. Instrument readings have to be changed to appropriate qualitative equivalents. In some cases, that can be a good deal of work. Take the case of the ABS system discussed in Section 6.1. The example of yawing given in Section 6.1 has one wheel speed increasing while the other is decreasing. In order to detect that, it would be necessary to extract two separate velocity trends. The work of interpreting trends from the data can be the most challenging part of building such systems.

The most promising applications of qualitative reasoning to real-time diagnostic problems have been in the areas of electrical power distribution grids and telecommunications networks. In both of these application areas, there are real advantages in being able to reason about the structure of the domain. This is because it changes comparatively frequently – because of physical reconfiguration of the grid as well as because of failures. The reconfiguration means that neural networks would have to be retrained, and rules would have to be rewritten. Quantitative models cannot be joined compositionally for diagnosis in the same way as qualitative models. Qualitative models, given a description of component behavior and the structure of the network can be used to interpret a series of network problem reports and to identify the source of the original network problem.

7.4 Commercial Real-Time Tools

The main toolkits used at present for building real-time systems are a mixture of tools for interface building, data monitoring and rule-based fault diagnosis. This section will describe the main features of one such tool, G2 from Gensym. Several other tools, such as COGSYS, offer similar features, but G2 has been around a long time and has perhaps the most fully developed set of tools for building real-time diagnostic systems. The major uses of such tools have been in large manufacturing plants – chemical processing plants, steel mills etc., and so when the different features of the toolkit are discussed, examples from that kind of application will be given.

7.4.1 Data Collection and Analysis Tools

One of the big issues when building a diagnostic system in a manufacturing plant is deciding on what computer the diagnostic system will run and from where it will get its data. When a plant has already been designed and built, and the plant control and data logging facilities are working satisfactorily, plant management will be very reluctant to change the arrangements for those facilities significantly. In particular, they are unlikely to agree to the diagnostic system running on the same computer(s) as the existing control and data logging tools. This follows the well-tried rule "if it isn't broken, don't fix it".

A frequent compromise is to take an existing data feed from a PLC (programmable logic controller), or to add an extra PC in the control room for the diagnostic system, communicating with the existing data-logging computers. In order to implement this solution, it is necessary to write software to communicate with other platforms and to perform the regular repeated data exchange. G2 provides facilities for this kind of data exchange for many common PLCs and computing platforms. Another excellent feature is the existence of database bridges, so that important events can be logged in a very usable way.

All of the data collection features of G2 are encapsulated as *G2 Gateway*. This can run on the same computer as G2, or can itself be run on a separate machine or network of machines. This means that G2 can be configured in an appropriate way to respond to the real-time needs of the particular diagnostic application being built. G2 Gateway can also communicate with tasks implemented in C++ or Java, so where computationally intense pre-processing of data is needed, it can be done more appropriately in C++ than in G2 itself. In the steel mill example given in Table 7.1 (implemented in COGSYS rather than G2), the pre-processing of individual data values into symbols such as SPIKES was done by this method.

All data collected by G2 is date stamped, so it is possible to reason about the relationship between a series of readings or alarms. This is vital for two reasons. For data, it allows the collation of a series of readings into a trend. For alarms, it enables reasoning about the relationship between alarms. Consider the case of the Three Mile Island reactor. One of the contributing factors to the problem was information overload. Operators failed to see a display showing a sensor failure among the many displays with which they were presented. They were confronted with over 100 alarms at once, and failed to figure out which was the appropriate one to respond to. Time signatures on alarms allow the system to calculate relationships between alarms, and present the plant engineer with an interpretation of the relationship between the alarms, highlighting the alarms that most probably provoked the alarm cascade. Sometimes, this interpreting facility of the on-line diagnostic system is more important than being able to decide on a root cause for the problem – given the correct information in a clear manner, the plant engineers are often capable of identifying the root cause for themselves.

7.4.2 Representation and Reasoning

G2 has an object-oriented representation, and so it is possible to describe plant items (pipes, containers) as objects. These objects can be linked, and so the diagnostic system can reason about the relationships between objects for consistency checks. For example, this pipe is connected to that tank, and so if the flow in the pipe is known, then the expected increase in fluid in the tank can be calculated and checked. This falls short of the kind of model-based reasoning described in Chapters 5 and 6, but can be very useful for detecting discrepancies. The object-oriented nature of the representation also saves effort, because objects of the same type only have to have their details described once. So, for example, in the steel mill example mentioned earlier, a press in the mill would be declared with certain features, and then several presses of the same type would be instantiated. This was also the case using the COGSYS language in the example given in Table 7.1. Data from the plant will tend to be associated with specific objects (such as flow in a pipe). When the data is read from the plant, it is either passed to the appropriate data objects, or an abstraction of it is passed. So, in the steel mill example in COGSYS, given earlier, the data about pressure readings on a press was abstracted to a trend, either NORMAL, SPIKES, or one of several other trends.

Once the representation has been declared, including relevant plant readings or abstractions of plant readings, it is possible to write rules that reason about the representation and the data. G2 rules are quite similar to the COGSYS rule given earlier, although a syntax directed editor restricts what rules can be given, while allowing a rather more English-like syntax. Table 7.2 shows an example G2 rule.

Acidity Rule
IF the standard deviation of the ph-value of any tank T during the last 5 minutes > .15
THEN
    conclude that the alarm-status of T is unstable-ph and start alarm-procedure (PH, T)
    and invoke ph-diagnostic rules

Table 7.2 G2 rule for checking tank pH levels.

Gensym also provides a neural network tool that can be used with G2, called NeurOn-Line. It can be used for problem detection in the kind of way described in Section 7.2.4. In the context of G2, it can also be used in a slightly different way. A net could be taught to recognize trends in different data, and so could be taught to recognize the NORMAL and SPIKES values for the pressure on the steel press from the raw data.

7.4.3 Graphical Data Presentation

It was observed earlier that providing the operator with information relevant to the diagnostic situation in a clear manner is often the most useful contribution that a diagnostic system can make in a difficult situation. For that reason, the user interface facilities are among the most important aspects of real-time diagnostic systems. Where objects in the representation also have a graphical depiction, that depiction can be linked to the values of the object. So, for example, where a tank has a level sensor, the picture of the tank could reflect the present level of the liquid in the tank. Where the tank level goes below the minimum level, the color of the tank could be changed to red to reflect that there is a problem on the plant.

Where plant displays already exist, then at least one of the diagnostic system displays should be built to be as similar as possible to it, but with the ability to reflect the extra information available within the diagnostic system. G2 provides primitives for other displays as well, such as displays showing trends on data, or the likely relationships between alarms that have occurred, or ordered lists of significant recent deviations from expected behavior.

The wide set of features provided by tools such as G2 mean that it is applicable to wider real-time tasks not just diagnosis, and Gensym quote example applications in the following areas:

- *Quality management:* essentially a problem detection system – detect when quality diverges from acceptable levels and take action.
- *Process optimization:* monitor and control a process so that maximum output levels are maintained.
- *Dynamic scheduling:* as demands change, replan to meet those demands.

7.5 Tiger: Diagnosing Gas Turbines

Tiger was a European Community funded project to explore the issues involved in building more advanced real-time toolkits. It concentrated on the difficult but potentially profitable task of diagnosing problems on gas turbines like the one shown in Figure 7.1. These are large energy generation systems primarily used to power process plants of power stations. The exhaust gas is hot enough to generate high-pressure steam. The steam is then used by processes, such as a large chemical plant, or to provide the steam for paper mills. In other cases, the steam powers a steam turbine driven generator, producing even more electricity for the same money.

Gas turbines tend to have hard-wired problem detection, and so the main challenge is to reason about the cause of an automatic shutdown, and then decide what needs to be done in order to make it safe to restart the turbine. Downtime for the gas turbine can also mean downtime for the factory powered by the turbine, and so an extended downtime affects the owner's profits very badly.

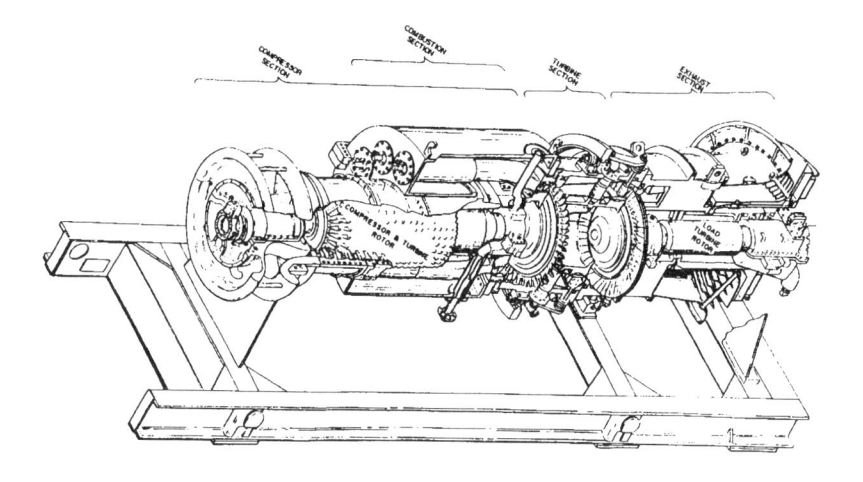

Fig. 7.1 Main components of a gas turbine.

The Tiger project (Milne *et al.*, 1996) focused on assembling an appropriate variety of the techniques discussed in this chapter and applying them to diagnosis on real gas turbines. The main techniques applied in Tiger were:

- real-time data acquisition;
- rule-based data interpretation;
- scenario detection tool;
- model-based diagnostic system;
- on-line alarm recording and interpretation.

7.5.1 Real-Time Data Acquisition

Tiger runs on a separate computer that communicates with the turbine control computer. Up to 750 different readings can be permanently recorded each second. Without interfering with the recording of new data, engineers are able to examine graphs of past data over periods between four minutes and several years. This enables the engineers to obtain a picture of trends over whatever time-scale they are interested in. The information can also be communicated with remote computers, so that turbine experts elsewhere can examine the data concerned with a particularly difficult turbine failure. As well as graphs of relevant data, Tiger provides an animated plant schematic view, showing the state of the plant.

The availability of clear incident data, and the ability to query it in different ways is itself an important tool for the engineers trying to fix the turbine, even if the rest of the abilities of Tiger were not available. One of the worst problems in gas turbine diagnosis has been trying to diagnose without complete information.

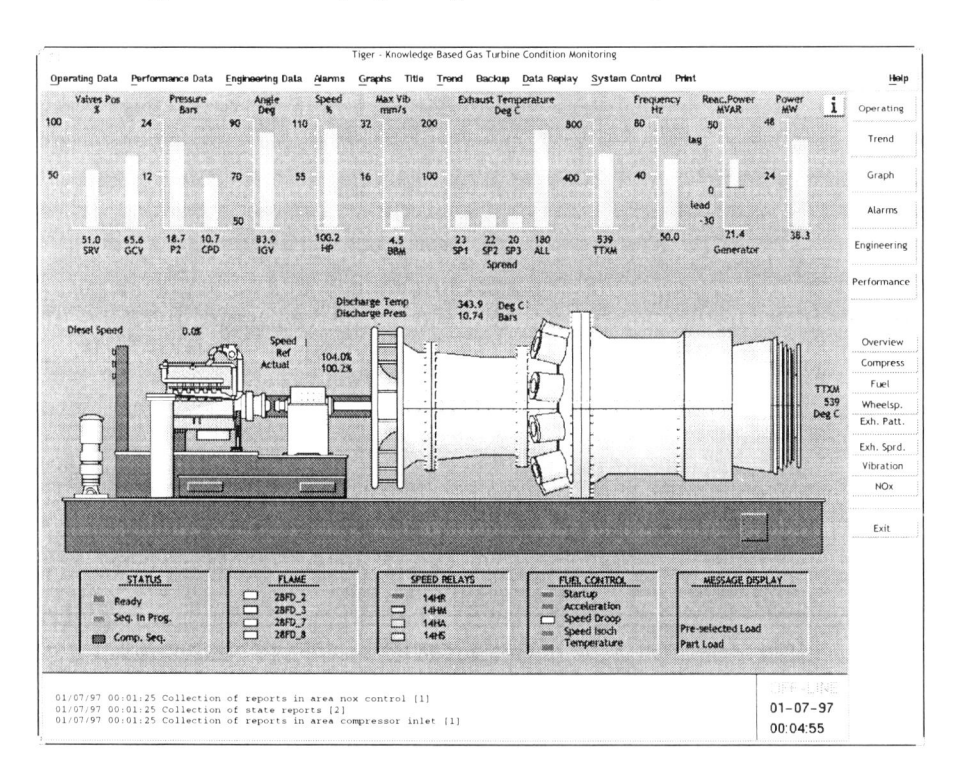

Fig. 7.2 Tiger monitoring turbine state.

7.5.2 Rule-Based Data Interpretation

As in G2 and COGSYS, rules can be used both for assembling a series of readings on a single sensor into a trend, and also for reasoning about the interactions between different sensors on the turbine. The rule-based engine compiles rules into a format that provides guarantees on the maximum response time of the rule base.

7.5.3 Scenario Detection Tool

Facilities are provided for the diagnostic system builder to describe sequences of events that can occur on the plant which either correspond to a particular failure occurring or to correct behavior. This is rather like a sequenced version of the instantaneous scenario descriptions used in RAZ'R (described in Section 6.1). These scenarios can be used to immediately characterize a problem as being caused by a particular fault. The scenario detection tool is able to reason about temporal sequences of events, and to recognize a series of events on the plant as equivalent to a series of events described as a scenario.

7.5.4 Model-Based Diagnostic System

Where equations of turbine behavior are available, they can be used to propagate values through the turbine. Where equations are not available, it is possible to represent the relationship between values causally (saying, for example, that when the pressure at sensor 23 increases rapidly, then the pressure at sensor 24 also will increase rapidly). Such descriptions can also include time delays (when the pressure increases at sensor 23, then it will increase at sensor 24 approximately 5 seconds later). The model-based part of Tiger can perform consistency-based diagnosis in the same kind of way as the RAZ'R system. It simulates the expected behavior of the system given the observed values in the system, and can then identify which components might be responsible for deviations from the expected behavior. The simulation engine for Tiger is based on intervals: rather than reasoning about numeric values or about completely qualitative values, it reasons about allowable envelopes within which calculated values should lie.

Typically, models that can be used for this kind of monitoring are only valid for stable operating conditions. In practice, this means that such models are unlikely to be valid during the start-up phase for the turbine, and during that phase, it is necessary to rely on the scenario detection tool to provide monitoring.

7.5.5 On-line Alarm Recording and Interpretation

The Tiger fault manager software co-ordinates all of the different modules of the Tiger turbine diagnostic system. It logs all alarms reported on the turbine, and highlights the alarms that the rules identify as the significant ones.

These facilities allow the turbine engineers to assess the overall state of the turbine and identify the real problems without wading through large numbers of fault reports. Figure 7.3 shows the contents of a Tiger screen informing the user about the cause of a turbine trip.

The turbine engineers can click on the significant alarm and receive data trends for the significant plant parameters during the period under question. The fault manager also provides its own interpretation of why the alarm occurred, provided by its fault diagnosis facilities. Finally, Tiger also provides on-line access to plant manuals, to assist in the turbine repair.

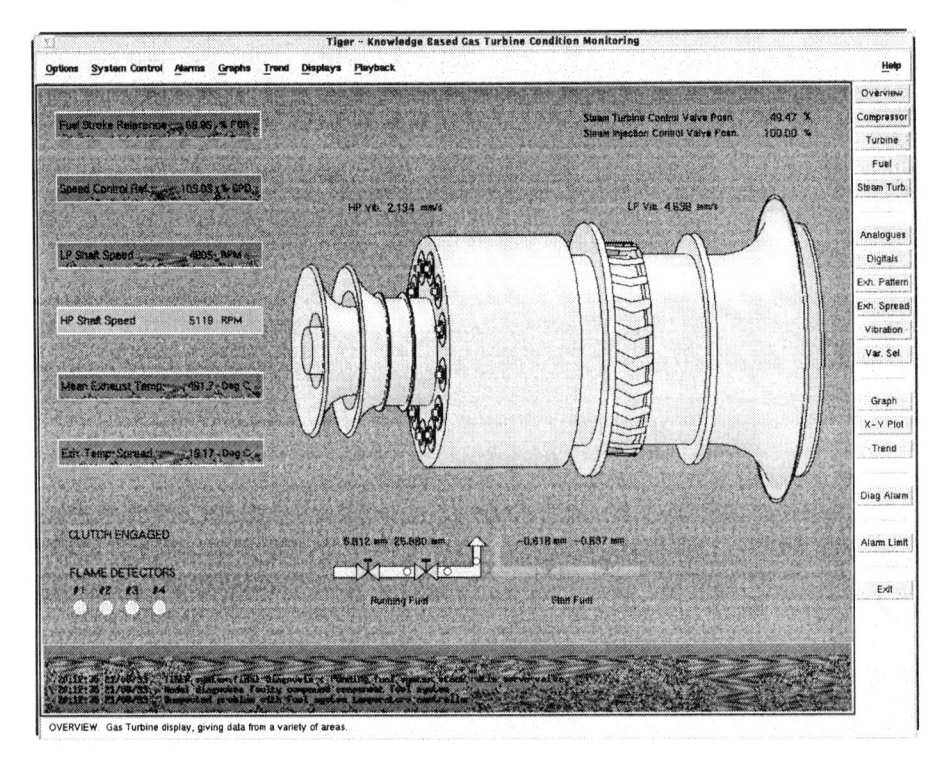

Fig. 7.3 Example Tiger fault screen.

7.5.6 Effectiveness of Tiger

One of the original plants used as a Tiger case study was a 25 megawatt gas turbine at Exxon's Fife Ethylene plant. If the turbine failed, then the plant had to be shut down, and so the turbine was a vital piece of equipment to the successful operation of the plant. After three years of operating this plant with the assistance of Tiger, the major benefits of deploying Tiger were seen as:

- *Reduced downtime.* Downtime was reduced, because of the rapid fault identification that was provided by Tiger when a problem occurred.
- *Avoidance of downtime.* This was achieved by recognizing incipient problems before they could cause a shutdown, and handling them in routine maintenance periods.

- *More effective monitoring.* The support provided by Tiger meant that there was better monitoring of the turbine when the most experienced engineers were not available.

One of the longer term outcomes of the Tiger project has been a commercial gas turbine diagnosis tool, also called Tiger. Kvaerner Energy have been selling this tool as an aid to remote diagnostic support for some time, and it has been running on a number of gas turbines with very positive results.

When Tiger is deployed on a new turbine, there is a short period of configuring the tool to match the structure of the new turbine, followed by several weeks of tuning the Tiger system to the actual running characteristics of the turbine. Compared with building a turbine diagnostic system from a general real-time diagnostic tool, this is a very short period indeed.

All data on the turbine is logged, and is available to experts at Kvaerner's support centre in Scotland. The availability of all data along with Tiger's conclusions on the causes of alarms and details of potential problems on the plant are available remotely to Kvaerner's experts as well as to the plant operators. One of the effects of this remote availability of all significant data is to make remote support much more effective.

Kvaerner give an example of a failure at a National Power turbine in the south of England. The failure was serious enough that before Tiger existed, they would have had to fly a turbine expert from Scotland to the turbine, resulting in an 8-10 hour delay before the turbine could be restarted. Examining the turbine data remotely, Kvaerner's turbine experts were able to identify the problem conclusively, and decide that the turbine could be restarted safely. The incident was then encoded into a new scenario, so that it could in future be recognized by Tiger without intervention from the expert.

Because each Tiger installation has basically the same software, tuned for that particular turbine, when new types of failure are found, rules to detect that kind of failure can be written and deployed to all Tiger users. The pooled experience of all Tiger users provides a richer diagnostic system than any one user might build on their own.

Appendix 1

Full Listing of Adviser Expert System

Model Simple_car_diagnosis
VERSION "1   5-May-92"
INTRO "!2N!T This expert system diagnoses car problems."

//*****
ACTION main_advice : "This action gives the diagnostic advice."
    PROVIDED NOT(car_starts)
    ADVISE "!2NThe problem seems to be ", answer, "!3N"

ACTION preliminary_reject : "Rejection at preliminary conditions."
    PROVIDED car_starts
    ADVISE "!5N This system is only designed for",
        "!N finding faults in cars that won't start."

//****** List of rules corresponding to each branching factor
STRING answer : "Top of the tree diagram: does the engine turn"
RULE a_answer : ""
    answer IS fuel_or_ign_fault
PROVIDED q_engine_turns
    ALSO answer IS st_motor_or_battery_fault
PROVIDED NOT(q_engine_turns)

STRING fuel_or_ign_fault: "No fuel or look at ignition or carb"
RULE a_fuel_or_ign_fault: ""
    fuel_or_ign_fault IS tank_empty
PROVIDED q_tank_empty
    ALSO fuel_or_ign_fault IS spark_or_carb_fault
PROVIDED NOT(q_tank_empty)

STRING spark_or_carb_fault: "Either no spark or a fuel feed problem"
RULE a_spark_or_carb_fault: ""
    spark_or_carb_fault IS ign_fault
PROVIDED NOT(q_spark_at_plug)
    ALSO spark_or_carb_fault IS carb_or_timing_fault
PROVIDED (q_spark_at_plug)

STRING ign_fault: "Check for HT fault"
RULE a_HT_fault: ""
    ign_fault IS HT_fault
PROVIDED NOT(q_spark_at_coil)
    ALSO ign_fault IS LT_fault
PROVIDED q_spark_at_coil

```
STRING carb_or_timing_fault: "Either no fuel at plug or no spark"
RULE a_carb_or_timing_fault: ""
    carb_or_timing_fault IS carb_or_line_fault
PROVIDED NOT(q_fuel_at_plug)
    ALSO carb_or_timing_fault IS timing_fault
PROVIDED (q_fuel_at_plug)

STRING carb_or_line_fault: "Either carburettor or fuel line problem"
RULE a_carb_or_line_fault: ""
    carb_or_line_fault IS carb_fault
PROVIDED q_fuel_at_carb
    ALSO carb_or_line_fault IS line_fault
PROVIDED NOT(q_fuel_at_carb)

STRING st_motor_or_battery_fault: ""
RULE a_st_motor_or_battery_fault: ""
    st_motor_or_battery_fault IS st_motor_fault
PROVIDED NOT(q_battery_flat)
    ALSO st_motor_or_battery_fault IS battery_fault
PROVIDED (q_battery_flat)

//***** List of questions corresponding to each branching factor
//************************************************

ASSERTION car_starts : "The user does not have a suitable problem"
    DEFAULT FALSE
QUESTION ask_if_car_starts: ""
    OBTAIN car_starts YESNO
    WITH "Try to start your car: did it start?"
    WHY "The system is only designed for no start problems."

ASSERTION q_engine_turns: ""
QUESTION ask_if_engine_turns: ""
    ANSWERS q_engine_turns
        CHOICE "No"           : FALSE
        CHOICE "Yes, but slowly": FALSE
        CHOICE "Yes, normally"  :TRUE
    WITH "Does the engine turn over? "

ASSERTION q_tank_empty : "the fuel tank is empty"
ASKABLE YESNO
    WHY "No fuel, then the car won't start."

ASSERTION q_spark_at_plug: "there is a spark at the plug"
ASKABLE YESNO
    WHY "No spark indicates an ignition fault."

ASSERTION q_spark_at_coil: "there is a spark at HT side of the coil"
ASKABLE YESNO
    WHY "No spark at coil indicates that it may be faulty, ",
        "or that it is not receiving power."
ASSERTION q_lamp_brightness: ""
QUESTION ask_how_bright_headlamps: ""
    ANSWERS q_lamp_brightness
        CHOICE "No light"         : FALSE
```

Appendix 1: Full Listing of Adviser Expert System

```
            CHOICE "Dim"            : FALSE
            CHOICE "Normal brightness ": TRUE
        WITH "How bright are the headlamps?"

ASSERTION q_battery_flat: ""
RULE a_battery_flat: ""
    q_battery_flat IS TRUE
        PROVIDED NOT(q_lamp_brightness)
    ALSO q_battery_flat IS FALSE
        PROVIDED (q_lamp_brightness)

ASSERTION q_fuel_at_plug: "fuel is reaching the plugs"
ASKABLE YESNO
    WHY "No fuel at plugs indicates a fuel line/carburettor fault."

ASSERTION q_fuel_at_carb: "fuel at the carburettor"
ASKABLE YESNO
    WHY "No fuel at the carburettor indicates a fuel line blockage."

//***** List of diagnoses and recommendations. ****************

CONSTANT STRING tank_empty = "that the car has no fuel."
            + "!2N Try filling up the tank."

CONSTANT STRING HT_fault = "in the HT circuit."
            + "!2N Check the HT leads and the distributor cap."

CONSTANT STRING LT_fault = "in the LT circuit."
            + "!2N Check the coil connections, "
            + "the points, and the coil."

CONSTANT STRING carb_fault = "a carburettor fault."
            + "!2N Check if the carburettor is blocked."

CONSTANT STRING timing_fault = "a timing fault."
            + "!2N Check the timing (or get a garage to do it)."

CONSTANT STRING st_motor_fault = "a starter motor fault."
            + "!2N Check the starter motor."

CONSTANT STRING battery_fault = "a flat battery."
            + "!2N Recharge the battery and figure out "
            + "why it was flat (lights on, old battery etc)."

CONSTANT STRING line_fault = "a fuel line blockage."
            + "!2N Check the fuel filter for blockage, "
            + "and the fuel line for leaks or kinks."
//===============================================================
```

The diagnostic example is one of a number of examples that have been implemented in the Adviser expert system, and so there is a preliminary exchange to choose the car diagnosis system. Two separate examples of using the car diagnostic system are shown here.

//   Adviser Expert System Executive, Augusta Technology 1994

//   Installation Reference : Chris Price - his copy

// If you do not know what to do at any time, type HELP.

// Current model is demo.mdl
// Version 1 4th July 1992
// Compiled at 04-Feb-95 16:38

Which of the following demos would you like to try?
1. PC hardware selection
2. Application form sifting
3. Personality test
4. Choosing a pet
5. Sportscar selection
6. Simple car diagnosis
7. Child health advice
8. Uni matric rules
(Please make your choice): **6**

// Current model is eg6.mdl
// Version 1 5-May-92
// Compiled at 04-Feb-95 16:11
   Type BEGIN to begin.

Command from command file : **begin**

       This expert system diagnoses car problems,

Try to start your car: did it start?
(You may answer Yes or No): **n**

Does the engine turn over?
1. No
2. Yes, but slowly
3. Yes, normally
(Please make your choice): **1**

How bright are the headlamps?
1. No light
2. Dim
3. Normal brightness
(Please make your choice): **1**

The problem seems to be a flat battery.

Recharge the battery and figure out why it was flat (lights on, old battery etc).

What would you like to do next?
1. Start this demo again
2. Go back to demo menu
3. Quit from Adviser
(Please make your choice): **1**

       This expert system diagnoses car problems,

Try to start your car: did it start?
(You may answer Yes or No): **n**

Appendix 1: Full Listing of Adviser Expert System

Does the engine turn over?
1. No
2. Yes, but slowly
3. Yes, normally
(Please make your choice): **3**

Is it true that the fuel tank is empty ?
(You may answer Yes or No): **n**

Is it true that there is a spark at the plug ?
(You may answer Yes or No): **n**

Is it true that there is a spark at HT side of the coil ?
(You may answer Yes or No): **y**

The problem seems to be in the LT circuit.
Check the coil connections, the points, and the coil.

Appendix 2

Details of GRAF2 Generated Programs

This appendix contains example Pascal and C programs generated by GRAF2 for the simple car diagnosis example described in Chapter 1. GRAF2 can be obtained from the Web site supporting this book.

Pascal Code Generated for Car Diagnosis Application

```
Program Diag;
var dummy: boolean;

procedure proc0;
begin
    writeln;
    writeln( 'No advice on this branch.');
    writeln;
end;

procedure proc16;
begin
    writeln( 'Sorry, only do non-starting' );
    writeln;
end;

procedure proc2;
begin
    writeln( 'Carburettor problem' );
    writeln;
end;

procedure proc1;
begin
    writeln( 'Blockage in fuel line' );
    writeln;
end;

procedure proc6;
var ch: Char;
begin
    write( 'Is fuel reaching the carburettor? ' );
```

```
    readln( Ch );
    writeln;
    if (ch = 'Y') OR (ch = 'y')
        then proc2
        else proc1;
end;

procedure proc5;
begin
    writeln( 'Problem with timing' );
    writeln;
end;

procedure proc8;
var ch: Char;
begin
    write( 'Is fuel reaching the plugs? ' );
    readln( Ch );
    writeln;
    if (ch = 'Y') OR (ch = 'y')
        then proc6
        else proc5;
end;

procedure proc4;
begin
    writeln( 'Fault in the LT circuit' );
    writeln;
end;

procedure proc3;
begin
    writeln( 'Fault in the HT circuit' );
    writeln;
end;

procedure proc7;
var ch: Char;
begin
    write( 'Spark at coil? ' );
    readln( Ch );
    writeln;
    if (ch = 'Y') OR (ch = 'y')
        then proc4
        else proc3;
end;

procedure proc9;
var ch: Char;
begin
    write( 'Spark at plug? ' );
    readln( Ch );
    writeln;
    if (ch = 'Y') OR (ch = 'y')
```

Appendix 2: Details of GRAF2 Generated Programs 135

```
            then proc8
            else proc7;
end;

procedure proc10;
begin
    writeln( 'Fill the tank' );
    writeln;
end;

procedure proc14;
var ch: Char;
begin
    write( 'Is there petrol? ' );
    readln( Ch );
    writeln;
    if (ch = 'Y') OR (ch = 'y')
        then proc9
        else proc10;
end;

procedure proc12;
begin
    writeln( 'Starter motor problem' );
    writeln;
end;

procedure proc11;
begin
    writeln( 'Flat battery problem' );
    writeln;
end;

procedure proc13;
var ch: Char;
begin
    write( 'Headlights working OK? ' );
    readln( Ch );
    writeln;
    if (ch = 'Y') OR (ch = 'y')
        then proc12
        else proc11;
end;

procedure proc15;
var ch: Char;
begin
    write( 'Does starter turn? ' );
    readln( Ch );
    writeln;
    if (ch = 'Y') OR (ch = 'y')
        then proc14
        else proc13;
end;
```

```pascal
procedure proc17;
var ch: Char;
begin
    write( 'Car starts? ' );
    readln( Ch );
    writeln;
    if (ch = 'Y') OR (ch = 'y')
        then proc16
        else proc15;
end;

begin
    writeln;
    proc17;
    readln;
end.
```

C Code Generated for Car Diagnosis Application

```c
#include <stdio.h>
#include <stdlib.h>
#include <string.h>
#include <time.h>

void proc16(void);
void proc2(void);
void proc1(void);
void proc6(void);
void proc5(void);
void proc8(void);
void proc4(void);
void proc3(void);
void proc7(void);
void proc9(void);
void proc10(void);
void proc14(void);
void proc12(void);
void proc11(void);
void proc13(void);
void proc15(void);
void proc17(void);
int yesOrNo(const char *prompt);
void skipToEOL(int c);

const int YES = 1, NO = 0;

int main()
{
    printf ("Starting diagnosis...\n\n");
    /* Call top node of tree */
```

Appendix 2: Details of GRAF2 Generated Programs

```
    proc17();
    printf("\n");
    return EXIT_SUCCESS;
}
int yesOrNo(const char *prompt)
{
    int answer = 0;
    while (printf(prompt), (answer = getchar()) != EOF)
    {
        skipToEOL( answer );
        if ((answer == 'y') || (answer == 'Y'))
            {return YES;}
        else
            {return NO; }
    }
    return NO;
    }
void skipToEOL(int c)
{
    while (c != '\n' && c != EOF)
        c = getchar();
}

void proc16(void)
{
    printf( "Sorry, only do non-starting\n");
}

void proc2(void)
{
    printf( "Carburettor problem\n");
}

void proc1(void)
{
    printf( "Blockage in fuel line\n");
}

void proc6(void)
{
    int answer;
    char *q;
    q = "Is fuel reaching the carburettor? ";
    answer = yesOrNo(q);
    printf("\n");
    if (answer == YES)
        proc2();
    else proc1();
}

void proc5(void)
{
```

```c
    printf( "Problem with timing\n");
}

void proc8(void)
{
    int answer;
    char *q;
    q = "Is fuel reaching the plugs? ";
    answer = yesOrNo(q);
    printf("\n");
    if (answer == YES)
        proc6();
    else proc5();
}

void proc4(void)
{
    printf( "Fault in the LT circuit\n");
}

void proc3(void)
{
    printf( "Fault in the HT circuit\n");
}

void proc7(void)
{
    int answer;
    char *q;
    q = "Spark at coil? ";
    answer = yesOrNo(q);
    printf("\n");
    if (answer == YES)
        proc4();
    else proc3();
}

void proc9(void)
{
    int answer;
    char *q;
    q = "Spark at plug? ";
    answer = yesOrNo(q);
    printf("\n");
    if (answer == YES)
        proc8();
    else proc7();
}

void proc10(void)
{
    printf( "Fill the tank\n");
}
```

Appendix 2: Details of GRAF2 Generated Programs

```
void proc14(void)
{
    int answer;
    char *q;
    q = "Is there petrol? ";
    answer = yesOrNo(q);
    printf("\n");
    if (answer == YES)
        proc9();
    else proc10();
}

void proc12(void)
{
    printf( "Starter motor problem\n");
}

void proc11(void)
{
    printf( "Flat battery problem\n");
}

void proc13(void)
{
    int answer;
    char *q;
    q = "Headlights working OK? ";
    answer = yesOrNo(q);
    printf("\n");
    if (answer == YES)
        proc12();
    else proc11();
}

void proc15(void)
{
    int answer;
    char *q;
    q = "Does starter turn? ";
    answer = yesOrNo(q);
    printf("\n");
    if (answer == YES)
        proc14();
    else proc13();
}

void proc17(void)
{
    int answer;
    char *q;
    q = "Car starts? ";
    answer = yesOrNo(q);
    printf("\n");
    if (answer == YES)
```

```
      proc16();
   else proc15();
}
```

Execution of Text-Based Car Diagnosis Application

When either the Pascal or C code above is compiled and run, then a dialogue of the following kind ensues:

Car starts? **N**

Does starter turn? **N**

Headlights working OK? **Y**

Starter motor problem

A different consultation with the same system might look like this.

Car starts? **N**

Does starter turn? **Y**

Is there petrol? **Y**

Spark at plug? **Y**

Is fuel reaching the plugs? **Y**

Is fuel reaching the carburettor? **N**

Blockage in fuel line

Execution of PalmPilot-Based Car Diagnosis Application

In the case of the PalmPilot, the generated code looks similar to the Pascal code, However, the PalmPilot has a window-and-pen-based interface which takes quite a lot of setting up, and so the generated code is added to several hundred lines of support code before being compiled. The resulting program can then be downloaded to the PalmPilot during a routine synchronization.

When the program is run, each question is presented to the user as a single window where either yes or no can be selected with the pen. Figure A2.1 shows the carburettor question listed in the previous question, and Figure A2.2 shows the next screen if the user selects No as an answer to that question.

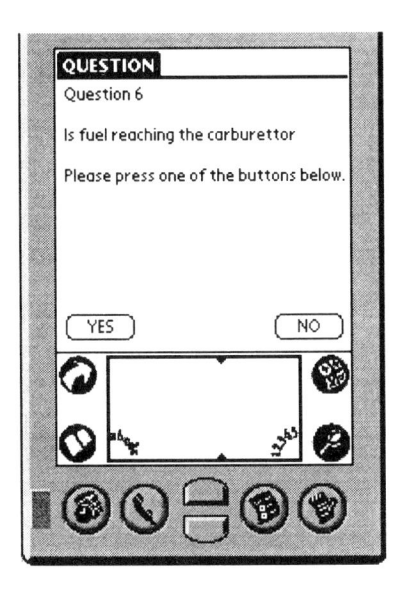

Appendix 2: Details of GRAF2 Generated Programs

Fig. A2.1 Question being asked by the PalmPilot diagnostic system.

Fig. A2.2 Advice being given by the PalmPilot diagnostic system.

Appendix 3

Further Information

This appendix contains a list of contacts and sources of information for tools of the types that are described in this book. The structure of this appendix follows the structure of the book.

Some of this information, especially Web and email addresses can change very quickly, and so up-to-date information is available on the Web site associated with the book. This can be found at "http:/www.aber.ac.uk/~cjp/diagnosticbook/".

Chapters 1 and 2: Rule-Based Diagnostic Tools

Software on the Web Site

The Adviser example diagnostic systems mentioned in Chapters 1 and 2, and the example in Appendix 1 can be loaded from the book-related Web site and run on a PC.

Intelligent Applications

Intelligent Applications are one of the oldest companies specializing in diagnostic systems. They have won several prizes in recognition of the diagnostic systems that they have built, and give details of a number of interesting systems and tools on their Web site.

Intelligent Applications Ltd
1 Michaelson Square
Livingston
West Lothian
Scotland
EH54 7DP, UK
Email: ia@intapp.co.uk
Web: http://www.intapp.co.uk/

Chapter 2: Diagnosability

Standards Details

Information about IEEE standards and about the Boundary Scan standard is available at the following sites.

IEEE http://www.ieee.org/index.html

http://www.computer.org/tab/tttc/standard/s1149-1/home.html

Diagnosability Research

Professor Robert Paasch at Oregon State University has done pioneering work in taking the concepts of diagnosability used in electronics and applying them to mechanical systems. Several papers written by him in association with his colleagues are available on his Web site at http://www.engr.orst.edu/~paasch/.

Chapter 3: Graphically Oriented Tool Builders

Software on the Web Site

A version of GRAF2 built in Borland Delphi can be loaded from the book-related Web site. It can generate diagnostic programs in Pascal or C that can be compiled and run on a PC. Alternatively, code can be generated for the 3Com PalmPilot, compiled and then downloaded to a PalmPilot or Palm III.

Carnegie Group

Carnegie Group specialize in consultancy, but have also built and sold the graphical tool TestBench, featured in Chapter 3.

Carnegie Group
Five PPG Place
Pittsburgh
PA 15222, USA
Tel: 1-412-642-6900
Tel: 1-800-284-3424
Fax: 1-412-642-6906
Email: info@cgi.com
Web: http://www.cgi.com/

Appendix 3: Further Information

GenRad

GenRad are a major supplier of automotive diagnostic systems, providing service bay diagnostic systems for customers such as Ford Motor Company Ltd.

GenRad
Orion Business Park
Bird Hall Lane
Stockport
SK3 0XG, UK
Tel: +44-161-491-9191
Fax: +44-161-491-9292
Web: http://www.genrad.com

Chapter 4: Case-Based Reasoning Tools

Software on the Web Site

The freeware CBR product, Caspian, is available on the book-related Web site. It is not particularly well suited for diagnostic applications, but a simple diagnostic application could be constructed using it.

Inference Corporation

Inference were one of the early names in diagnostic systems, with applications built in a tool called ART. CBR Express is widely used for help desk-based diagnostic help.

Inference Corp.
Tel: (415) 893-7200
Email: info@inference.com
Web: http://www.inference.com

Brightware, Inc.

Brightware have produced both CBR products and rule-based products such as ART*Enterprise. They presently position themselves as a "solutions" company, giving their CBR technology names like "Brightware answer agent" and "Brightware Advice agent".

Brightware Inc.
350 Ignacio Blvd.
Novato
CA 94949, USA
Tel: (800) 572-3675 or call (415) 884-4864
Fax: (415) 884-4740

Email: info@brightware.com
Web: http://www.brightware.com

Integrated Diagnostic System (IDS)

Further details of the IDS aircraft maintenance system described in Section 4.3 are available on the Web at http://ai.iit.nrc.ca/IR_public/ids/. This site is maintained by the National Research Council of Canada, who developed the system for Air Canada.

QPAC

Further details of the QPAC troubleshooting and process FMEA system are given on the Web at http://www.aber.ac.uk/~dcswww/Research/arg/QPAC/. Some of the QPAC software is also available on this site, although not the troubleshooting software at present.

Chapters 5 and 6: Model-Based Reasoning Tools

MONET

MONET is the European Network of Excellence in Model Based Systems and Qualitative Reasoning. It is tasked with promoting the technology to industry within Europe. Its Web site has information that should help those investigating the technology, and membership of the network is available to companies worldwide. They intend to make example model-based reasoning tools available on their Web site (http://monet.aber.ac.uk/) in the near future.

OCC'M

OCC'M are a start up company for exploiting model-based reasoning technology. They are responsible for the RAZ'R tool described in Section 6.1. They provide both tools and consultancy in this area.

OCC'M Software GmbH
Gleissentalstr. 22
82041 Deisenhofen
Germany
Tel. +49-89-613.46.98,
Fax +49-89-613.396.98
Email: contact@occm.de
Web: http://www.occm.de/

Appendix 3: Further Information

FirstEarth

FirstEarth is a start up company producing automated design analysis tools. Its main product at present is the AutoSteve tool for automating failure mode and effects analysis, using model-based simulation. It has also built diagnostic systems using the FMEA information, as detailed in Section 6.2.

FirstEarth Limited
53 Erw Goch
Waun Fawr
Aberystwyth
SY23 3AZ, UK
Email: autosteve-sales@autosteve.com
Web: http://www.autosteve.com

NASA

The model-based autonomous systems research group at NASA AMES is responsible for the autonomous spacecraft diagnostic work detailed in Section 6.3. Details of their work are on the Web at http://ic.arc.nasa.gov/ic/projects/mba/.

NorthWestern University

Profesor Ken Forbus and the Qualitative Reasoning Group at NorthWestern University have applied model-based reasoning to a number of interesting engineering problems, and make both information and software available on their Web site at http://www.qrg.ils.nwu.edu/.

University of Texas at Austin

The model-based reasoning group at UTA, run by Professor Ben Kuipers also makes information and model-based reasoning software available on their Web site at http://www.cs.utexas.edu/users/qr/.

Chapter 7: Real-Time Diagnostic Tools

Gensym Corporation

Gensym provides real-time expert systems for online applications. Their main product is the G2 real-time expert system product. It claims that there are over 1500 installations of G2 worldwide.

Gensym Corporation
125 Cambridge Park Drive
Cambridge
MA 02140, USA
Tel: (617) 547-2500
Fax: (617) 547-1962
Email: info@gensym.com
Web: http://www.gensym.com

Cogsys

Cogsys is a company that emerged from a collaborative real-time systems development project between 25 major companies in the mid 1980s. It specializes in the development and application of real-time, intelligent software systems. Its main product is the COGSYS toolkit for building applications to handle the rapid analysis of multiple data streams in real time.

Cogsys Ltd
26-28 Leslie Hough Way
Salford
M6 6AJ, UK
Tel: +44 (0)161 745 7604
Fax: + 44 (0)161 736 2634
Email: info@cogsys.co.uk
Web site: http://www.cogsys.co.uk/

Integrated Diagnostics Centre at Georgia Tech

Three universities, funded by the Office of Naval Research have established the "MultiUniversity Center for Integrated Diagnostics", based at Georgia Tech. The Center is designed to identify and exploit research opportunities associated with detecting incipient failures through real-time monitoring.

Web site: http://www.me.gatech.edu/Diagnostics

Intelligent Applications

Intelligent Applications have a long record of building real-time systems, including their work on Tiger, described in Chapter 7. Contact details are given earlier in this appendix.

Tiger

The Tiger system for monitoring gas turbines, described in Chapter 7, is now available commercially from Kvaerner Energy Limited.

Kvaerner Energy Limited
Tiger Support Desk
Thermal Power Division
John Brown Engineering Works
Clydebank
G81 1YA, UK
Tel: +44-141-305-4518
Fax: +44-141-952-8764
Email: tiger@traf.com

References

Acorn, T.L. and Walden, S.H. (1992) "SMART: Support Management Automated Reasoning Technology for Compaq Customer Service", in A.C. Scott and P. Klahr (eds.) *Innovative Applications of Artificial Intelligence 4*, AAAI Press, pp. 3-18.

Clark, G. and Paasch, R. (1996) "Diagnostic Modeling and Diagnosability Evaluation of Mechanical Systems", *Journal of Mechanical Design*, Vol. 118 (3), pp. 425-31.

Dattani, I, Magaldi, R.V. and Bramer, M.A. (1996) "A Review and Evaluation of the Application of Case-based Reasoning (CBR) Technology in Aircraft Maintenance", *Applications and Innovations in Expert Systems*, Vol. IV, pp. 189-203, SGES Publications.

Davis, R. (1984) "Diagnostic Reasoning Based on Structure and Behavior", *Artificial Intelligence*, Vol. 24 (3), pp. 347-410.

Davis, R. and Hamscher, W. (1992) "Model-Based Reasoning: Troubleshooting", in Hamscher *et al.* (1992).

de Kleer, J. and Brown, J.S. (1984) "A Qualitative Physics Based on Confluences", *Artificial Intelligence*, Vol. 24 (3), pp. 7-83.

de Kleer, J. and Williams, B. (1987) "Diagnosing Multiple Faults", *Artificial Intelligence*, Vol. 32, pp. 97-130.

Expert systems with applications special issue on case-based reasoning. *Expert Systems with Applications*, Vol. 6(1), 1993.

Forbus, K. (1990) "The Qualitative Process Engine", in D. Weld and J. de Kleer (eds.), *Readings in Qualitative Reasoning about Physical Systems*, Morgan Kaufmann, pp. 220-35.

Forbus, K. and Falkenhainer, B. (1990) "Self-explanatory Simulations: An Integration of Qualitative and Quantitative Knowledge", in *Proceedings AAAI-90*, AAAI Press, pp. 380-87.

Forbus, K. and Falkenhainer, B. (1992) "Self-explanatory Simulations: Scaling Up to Large Models", in *Proceedings AAAI-92*, AAAI Press, pp. 685-90.

Frank, P. (1990) "Fault Diagnosis in Dynamic Systems using Analytical and Knowledge-Based Redundancy", *Automatica*, Vol. 26, pp. 459-74.

Genesereth, M. (1984) "The Use of Design Descriptions in Automated Diagnosis", *Artificial Intelligence*, Vol. 24 (3), pp. 411-36.

Hammond, K. J. (1989) *Case-Based Planning*, Academic Press.

Hamscher, W., Console, L. and de Kleer, J. (1992) *Reasonings in Model-Based Diagnosis*, Morgan Kaufmann.

Hessel, G., Schmitt, W., van der Vorst, K., Weiss, F-P., Neumann, J., Schlüter, S. and Steiff, A. (1997) "Identification of Dangerous States in Chemical Batch Reactors using Neural Networks", in *Proceedings IFAC SafeProcess 97*, Hull, pp. 926-31.

IEEE Expert special issue on case-based reasoning, *IEEE Expert*, Vol. 7(5), October 1992, pp. 5-26.

Isermann, R. (1993) "Fault Diagnosis of Machines via Parameter Estimation and Knowledge Processing", *Automatica*, Vol. 29 (4), pp. 815-35.

Iwata, Y. and Obama, N. (1991) "QDES: Quality Design Expert Systems for Steel Products", in R.G. Smith and A.C. Scott (eds.) *Innovative Applications of Artificial Intelligence 3*, AAAI Press, pp. 177-91.

Kirkham, C. and Harris, T. (1997) "A Hybrid Neural Network System for Generic Bearing Fault Detection", in *Proceedings COMADEM 97*, Helsinki, June.

Kolodner, J.L. (1991) "Improving Human Decision Making through Case-Based Decision Aiding", *AI Magazine*, Vol. 12 (2), pp. 52-68.

Kolodner, J.L. (1992) "An Introduction to Case-Based Reasoning", *Artificial Intelligence Review*, Vol. 6(1), pp. 3-34.

Kolodner, J.L. (1993) *Case-Based Reasoning*, Morgan Kaufmann.

Köppen-Seliger, B. and Frank, P. (1996) "Neural Networks in Model-Based Fault Diagnosis", in *Proceedings of 13th Triennial IFAC World Congress*, San Francisco, Vol. 7, pp. 67-72.

Kriegsman, N. and Barletta, R. (1993) "Building a Case-Based Help Desk Application", *IEEE Expert*, December, pp. 18-26.

Magaldi, R. (1994) "Maintaining Aeroplanes in Time-Constrained Operational Situations using Case-Based Reasoning", in J.M. Haton, M. Keane and M. Manago (eds.) *Advances in Case-Based Reasoning*, Springer-Verlag.

Marir, F. and Watson, I. (1994) "Case-Based Reasoning: A Categorized Review", *Knowledge Engineering Review*, Vol. 9(4), pp. 355-81.

Milne, R., Travé-Massuyès, L. and Quevedo, J. (1996) "Tiger: Numeric and Qualitative Model Based Diagnosis", in *Proceedings of 13th Triennial IFAC World Congress*, Elsevier, San Francisco, Vol. 7, pp. 127-32.

Nguyen, T., Czerwinski, M. and Lee, D. (1993) "COMPAQ QuickSource: Providing the Consumer with the Power of Artificial Intelligence", *Proceedings of the 5th Innovative Applications of Artificial Intelligence Conference*, Washington, DC, pp. 142-51.

Patton, R., Frank P. and Clark, R. (eds.) (1989) *Fault Diagnosis in Dynamic Systems: Theory and Applications*, Prentice-Hall.

Pegah, M., Bond, W. and Sticklen, J. (1993) "Representing and Reasoning about the Fuel System of the McDonnell Douglas F/A-18 from a Functional Perspective", *IEEE Expert*, Vol. 8 (2), pp. 65-71.

Preist, C. and Welham, B. (1990) "Modelling Bridge Faults for Diagnosis in Electronic Circuits", in *Proceedings of the First International Workshop on Principles of Diagnosis*, Stanford.

Price, C. (1996) "Effortless Incremental Design FMEA", in *Proceedings of the Annual Reliability and Maintainability Symposium*, pp. 43-47.

Price, C. (1998) "Function-Directed Electrical Design Analysis", *Artificial Intelligence in Engineering*, Vol. 12(4), pp. 445-56.

Price, C. and Taylor, N. (1997) "Multiple Fault Diagnosis Using FMEA", in *Proceedings of the AAAI97/IAAI97*, Providence, Rhode Island, pp. 1052-57.

Rieger, C. and Grinberg, M. (1978) "A System of Cause-Effect Representation and Simulation for Computer-aided Design", in Latombe (ed.) *Artificial Intelligence and Pattern Recognition in Computer-aided Design*, North-Holland, pp. 299-333.

Sachenbacher, M., and Struss, P. (1997) "Fault Isolation in the Hydraulic Circuit of an ABS: A Real-World Reference Problem for Diagnosis", in *Working Notes of the 8th International Workshop on the Principles of Diagnosis, (DX-97)*, Mont-St-Michel, September, pp. 113-19.

Schenck, D. and Wilson, P. (1994) *Information Modeling the EXPRESS Way*, Oxford University Press.

Sticklen, J. (1987) "MDX2: An Integrated Medical Diagnostic System", PhD thesis, Ohio State University.

Struss, P. and Dressler, O. (1992) "Physical Negation: Integrating Fault Models into the General Diagnostic Engine", in Hamscher *et al.* (1992), pp. 153-58.

Watson, I. (1997) *Applying Case-Based Reasoning: Techniques for Enterprise Systems*, Morgan-Kaufmann.

Williams, B. and Nayak, P. (1996) "Immobile Robots: AI in the New Millennium", *AI Magazine*, Vol. 17 (3), pp. 16-35.

Wylie, R., Orchard, R., Halasz, M. and Dubé, M. (1997) "IDS: Improving Aircraft Fleet Maintenance", *Proceedings of the AAAI97/IAAI97*, Providence, Rhode Island, pp. 1078-85.

Zhou, J. and Bennett, S. (1997) "Dynamic System Fault Diagnosis Based on Neural Network Modelling", in *Proceedings IFAC SafeProcess 97*, Hull, pp. 54-59.

Index

accessibility 24
Airbus diagnosis 56
anti-lock braking 90, 93–94, 114, 117
AutoSteve 95, 97–101, 103, 147

case-based reasoning 10, 30, 47–51, 53–56, 61–62, 64, 87, 115
CBR Express 49–54, 145
chemical plant 2, 10, 18, 21, 26, 66, 80, 83, 109–10, 118, 121
COGSYS 32, 116, 118–20, 122, 148
component-based model 76–77, 79–80, 84, 97
compositional modeling 80–81
cost/benefit ratio 2

dependency model 65, 67, 70–73, 80, 84
diagnosability 22–23, 26–27, 103, 144
diagnostic fault trees 2–11, 13–14, 16, 18, 20–22, 29–34, 38, 41–42, 45–46, 89, 96, 99, 102–103, 112, 115
diagnostic trouble codes 38–39, 46

expert system 1, 3, 4, 6–9, 13, 29, 47, 53, 127, 129–30, 147

fault diagnosis 18, 20, 22, 24, 33, 46, 48, 73, 83, 109, 114, 116, 118, 124
fault identification 18, 20, 22, 24, 33, 46, 68, 73, 77, 79–80, 83–84, 100, 117, 124
fault localization 18, 20, 22, 24, 33, 48, 68–69, 71, 73, 77, 83–84, 100, 109
fault models 66, 77–80, 95, 97
FMEA 22, 63–64, 93, 96–103, 112, 146–47
fuzzy reasoning 1

G2 118–20, 122, 147
gas turbines 66, 109, 121–22, 124–25, 149
GDE 89, 90, 95
GRADE™ 29, 37, 102
GRAF2 29–33, 35, 133, 144

hardware diagnosis 11, 37, 44, 46, 104, 130
HAZOP 22

helicopters 109–10, 113
help desk systems 11, 20, 49–50, 52, 54, 64

IDS application 55, 58, 146
interface 4, 6, 33, 35, 38, 40, 42, 45–46, 48, 50, 54, 118, 120, 140

maintainability 1, 8
medical diagnosis 1, 37
model-based diagnosis 10–11, 65, 71, 73, 80, 84, 86–87, 89, 95, 97, 102–104, 106–107, 111, 114–15, 117, 119, 123, 146–47
monitoring 11, 18–20, 38, 55, 57–58, 84, 104, 109–11, 113–16, 118, 122–23, 125, 148–49

NASA 103–104, 107, 147
neural networks 115, 117–18, 120

observability 24, 26
on-board diagnosis 19, 24, 38–40, 46, 56, 94, 103–104, 109–10, 113

PalmPilot 30–31, 140–41, 144
part replacement 1
problem identification 18–20, 33, 68–69, 71, 73, 77, 83–85, 110–11, 114

QuickSource 54

real-time diagnosis 12, 20, 84, 109–21, 125, 147–48
repair 4, 8, 18–20, 23–24, 30, 32–33, 40, 46, 50–51, 56, 58, 66, 124
response time 2, 123

safety critical 2, 55, 97, 115
scenario 30, 94, 106, 123, 125
SMART application 52–54
spacecraft diagnosis 103
state-based model 65, 73, 80, 84
state graph 71–73, 76–78
steel mill monitoring 109, 112–13, 116–19

155

suspect exoneration   69, 70, 73, 79, 101, 103
suspect generation   69, 73

testability   23–26
TestBench™   29, 33
TestBuilder™   33

Tiger   121–25, 148–49
troubleshooting   2–3, 13, 18–19, 21, 55, 58–60, 63–64, 146

Web material   143